A Live Theatre and Royal Court co-production

THE BOUNDS

by Stewart Pringle

Thursday 16 May – Saturday 8 June 2024
(Live Theatre, Newcastle)

Thursday 13 June – Saturday 13 July 2024
(Royal Court Theatre, London)

THE BOUNDS

by Stewart Pringle

CAST

Soroosh Lavasani
Ryan Nolan
Lauren Waine
Nathaniel Campbell-Goodwin (Live Theatre)
James Green (Live Theatre)
Wilbur Conabeare (Royal Court)
Harry Weston (Royal Court)

CREATIVE & PRODUCTION TEAM

Jack McNamara	Director
Verity Quinn	Designer
Drummond Orr	Lighting Designer
Matthew Tuckey	Sound Designer
Jayne Dent	Songwriter
Lou Duffy	Costume Supervisor
Craig Davidson	Stage Manager
Chloe Ribbens	Deputy Stage Manager
Drummond Orr	Production Manager
Taylor Howie	Technician
JD Stewart	Producer
Verity Naughton CDG	Casting Director (Royal Court for role of Boy)
Becky Morris	Audition Support (Live Theatre for role of Boy)
Alicia Meehan	Fight Director/Movement Director
Patrycja Nowacka	Prosthetic Design/Creation

A Word from Writer Stewart Pringle

In the Tudor House in Margate there is, or was, a small laminated slip of card on a notice board.

In metallic WordArt it reads 'Did You Know?' (it's for children, this notice board). 'Did You Know? Football was played in Tudor times. There were no set numbers of players in each team and the goal posts were a mile apart. It was very violent!'

Well, I didn't know. This was February 2018, I was having a weekend in Margate with my then-partner-now-wife Lauren, and I was vaguely looking for a new play to write. I'd just had the most exciting few months of my writing career, doing my first 'proper' play (ie: one I didn't have to do anything for other than write and then sit and enjoy), and I was looking for a new idea. And there it was – bang. A muddy field in the sixteenth century. Two young people playing football in the kind of positions me and my friends would be stuck in at school, in a huge game that could last for days and was 'very violent!' Writes itself. I didn't know much about football, but my very kind agent Jonathan agreed to take me to some QPR games. Magic! Next play sorted! Onwards!

Anyway, it didn't write itself. It wrote itself for about thirty pages and ran out of road. I was really pleased with my two characters, but I didn't have a story. I knew it wasn't going to be 'about' football, but what was it going to be about? So it sat in my Scripts folder, unloved, while I moved onto other things.

But then in 2020 the world as I had known it ended, or at least paused, and I came back to 'Tudor football idea D1.docx'. And suddenly it seemed to be 'about' all sorts of things. If you're anything like me you might be reading this note before the lights go down, on the Quayside or in Sloane Square or elsewhere, so I'll go easy on the spoilers, but the 'about'-ness of this play kept expanding. It became about violence and place and history. It became about friendship and love and village life and the landscape. And demons and faith and prophecy and deep time.

And then, inevitably, I suppose, it became about my life, and how I felt about the North, which I had all but left behind almost two decades ago, and still miss every single day. It became about all the things I love and hate and fear about the world, and largely about belonging, and loss. It became the most peculiar thing I'd ever written.

The world isn't always kind to peculiar things, so it was with immense delight and surprise that I heard that Jack was, and that Live Theatre were interested in bringing Percy, Rowan and Samuel to life. And then another round of delight and surprise when David told me the Court would like to meet them too. Actually writing plays has got a little crowded out of my life in recent years, and you always have that fear that it might get bustled out altogether, so this has been the most timely and exciting (and terrifying) bit of news.

Growing up in Northumberland, Live Theatre, along with Northern Stage and the Theatre Royal, was a revelatory place. I came on school trips, led by our extraordinary, effervescent and much missed drama teacher Mike Fry, but never dreamed I would be able to share a bit of my heart on its stage. And moving to London in 2010, the Royal Court was just what playwriting meant to me, for so long. It was where I came to see the most exciting and impossible ideas thrashed out in a public forum. It's where *The Rocky Horror Show* started for God's sake! So this has been an embarrassment of riches, really, and I'll never be able to express how grateful I am for it all.

I never know what a play will be about when I start it. My wife says that's 'discovery writing' but I suspect it may just be a lack of forward planning. But this started with an image, in a slightly dusty Margate museum: Percy and Rowan, on a muddy Northumbrian field. Me and my weird mates, playing 'defence' on the fringes of a muddy playing field in Haydon Bridge. My incredible family, living and loving and losing in the fields and fells and peat bogs that encircle the Allen Valleys. Mike Fry and his drama class, bending backwards and forwards in time, as the lights go down in Live, waiting for the story to begin.

S.P.
Penrith, March 2024

Director's Note

The Bounds has the unique honour of being the first production in Live Theatre's 51st birthday year. A year that deserves more press than it gets. We harped on about our 50th at the time, but surely it is surviving a milestone year and taking your first steps into an unburdened future that really counts. And how better to step into the future than to go back nearly five hundred years into the past? This might well be one of the only 'ancient' dramas Live Theatre has ever staged but it also feels like one of our most modern. And Stewart Pringle, like many masters of the uncanny, knows how to walk that line. He doesn't speak about where we are by grabbing shots of it on his phone but by digging into the ground beneath us to see what delights (and horrors) lie hidden. The deeper he tunnels the darker, the muddier. But also the closer he gets to bursting through a surface that looks uncannily like where we are now. Or where we might end up. Stewart's play feels haunted, but unlike your standard ghost story these apparitions come not from the past but from the future. Its characters know in their bones that changes are coming that may wipe them out of history. Yet they cling to their patch of earth, defiant, despairing and tragically optimistic. Like devoted fans resigned to watching their beloved team so nearly win and yet so eternally lose.

Jack McNamara,
Artistic Director of Live Theatre

BIOGRAPHIES

SOROOSH LAVASANI

Soroosh Lavasani graduated from the London Academy of Music and Dramatic Arts (LAMDA), and since then he has had the pleasure of working in a variety of incredible theatre shows, film, TV and video games. Previous work includes UK tours such as *The Kite Runner* and *Peter Pan Goes Wrong*, as well as great northern-based theatre such as *Our Laygate* at the Customs House Theatre. He's also thoroughly enjoyed his screen work in *Halbschatten* premiering at the Berlinale Film Festival, and will soon be appearing in Amazon Prime and Blumhouse's feature film *House of Spoils*. Video game characters including *Final Fantasy XVI*. Though he has performed a couple of readings for Live Theatre in the past (*The Filleting App*, *Snookered*) this will be his first play with the theatre, as well as his first play with the Royal Court. He would like to express his joy and love for both magical homes of storytelling.

RYAN NOLAN

Ryan is a native Geordie, who trained with Project A in Newcastle.

Ryan was most recently seen in a brand-new series for BBC One and BBC iPlayer, co-created by Bafta Award-winning writers Paul Coleman and Sian Gibson, *The Power of Parker*, playing the role of Liam.

He played Alfie in the one-man show *Father Unknown* at Gala Durham and Northern Stage, and prior to this he finished a run at Live Theatre Newcastle in *One Off*, playing the role of Brown.

Other theatre credits include: the role of Richard in Starz's *Becoming Elizabeth*, alongside a stellar cast including Bella Ramsey, Tom Cullen and Alicia von Rittberg; and the role of Skin-Lad/Curt in the 35th anniversary production of *Road* at Northern Stage, directed by the newly appointed AD of the theatre, Natalie Ibu.

Ryan filmed the role of Bixler on *Masters of The Air* for Apple TV and made his feature film debut as Private Malky in Sam Mendes' award winning *1917* (Dreamworks). Other film credits include *How To Build A Girl* (Film4).

TV credits include: *The Left Behind*, which won a BAFTA for Best Single Drama and *Casualty* (BBC).

LAUREN WAINE

Lauren is thrilled to be making her Live Theatre and Royal Court debut.

Lauren is an actor/facilitator from the North East with a wealth of experience in stage, screen and voiceover. She trained at LIPA and NYT.

Theatre credits: *Hey Diddle Diddle* (Kitchen Zoo); *No 9* (Northern Stage/ Alphabetti Theatre); *The Secret Garden* (tour); *Wor Bella* (NE tour); *The Snow Queen*, *The War of The Worlds* (Northern Stage); *The Importance of Being Earnest* (Hangfire Theatre); *Skellig* (Nottingham Playhouse); *Wormtown* (The Customs House/Alphabetti); *Faustus* (The Globe, Sam Wanamaker Festival); *Pericles* (Brighton Open Air Theatre).

TV/radio credits: *The World's Worst Dinner Party* (Channel 4); *The Dumping Ground* (CBBC); *Vera* (ITV); *The Infirmary* (Amazon/Audible).

Other: *Hylton*, *We Have a Problem* (Tiny Dragon Productions).

NATHANIEL CAMPBELL-GOODWIN (Live Theatre)

Nathaniel is in Year 5 at middle school and lives in Newcastle with his parents and big sister. He loves attending SA Youth Academy at weekends. He also enjoys playing football and rugby, and has recently begun learning to play Samba drums. He has been a supporting artist in the TV series *The Red King* and the film *A Mother for an Hour*. Nathaniel is thrilled to be making his professional debut in *The Bounds* at Live Theatre.

JAMES GREEN (Live Theatre)

James is currently a Year 5 pupil in a primary school in Gateshead. After being invited on stage from the audience during a pantomime as a very young boy, his love for performing grew. As part of Nice Swan Academy, he attends weekly singing lessons and, during the weekends, performing arts classes. He is learning the violin and enjoys singing. While James has performed in shows with his academy and in school, he is extremely proud to have secured his first professional role at Live Theatre in *The Bounds*.

WILBUR CONABEARE (Royal Court)

This is Wilbur's professional stage debut.

Television includes: *Brave Bunnies*, *Isadora Moon*, *Princess Mirror-Belle*.

HARRY WESTON (Royal Court)

Harry trains at D&B Academy of Performing Arts.

Theatre includes: *Standing at the Sky's Edge* (National Theatre); *Bach & Sons* (Bridge Theatre); *Leopoldstadt* (Sonia Friedman).

Television and animation includes: *Holby City* Series XXI, *Brave Bunnies*.

Film includes: *Do You See What I See*.

Creative & Production Team

STEWART PRINGLE | Writer

Stewart is a writer and dramaturg, born and raised in Allendale, Northumberland, and currently based in London. His work for the stage includes the Papatango Prize-winning *Trestle* (Southwark Playhouse), *The Ghost Hunter* (Old Red Lion Theatre, UK tour) and *The Horror! The Horror!* (w/ Tom Richards & Jeffrey Mayhew, Wilton's Music Hall). He is currently Senior Dramaturg at the National Theatre, and has previously worked as Associate Dramaturg at the Bush Theatre and Artistic Director of the Old Red Lion Theatre. Outside of the theatre he worked for many years as a culture journalist, and has written extensively in the Whoniverse for Big Finish Productions, usually with his wife Lauren Mooney.

JACK MCNAMARA | Director

Jack has been Artistic Director and Joint CEO of Live Theatre in Newcastle since 2021. Productions for the company as director include: *The Cold Buffet*, *We Are The Best!*, *One Off*. Previously he was Artistic Director of New Perspectives in Nottingham, where productions included: the multiple award-winning *The Fishermen* (West End, Home Manchester, BBC Radio 3, British Council Showcase); *The Lovesong of Alfred J Hitchcock* (Off Broadway); *The Boss of it All* (Soho Theatre/Offie Nominated); *Darkness Darkness* (Nottingham Playhouse) and first national tours of plays by Athol Fugard and debbie tucker green among many others. Recent freelance work includes *Shy* by Max Porter (Southbank Centre) starring Toby Jones and Ruth Wilson. He directed the epic audiobook *Voice of the Fire* by Alan Moore starring Maxine Peake, Mark Gatiss and Jason Williamson of Sleaford Mods.

VERITY QUINN | Designer

Verity is a set and costume designer for theatre and exhibition.

Selected credits include: *A Song for Ella Grey* (Pilot Theatre, Northern Stage and York Theatre Royal); *One Off* (Live Theatre and Paines Plough); *Tiny Fragments of Beautiful Light* (Allison Davies & Alphabetti Theatre); *Hidden Stories* exhibition (SeventeenNineteen, MishMash & Sunderland Music Hub); *Baby Show, Seesaw, Laika, Septimus Bean, Once Upon a Christmas, When I Think About the World I Laugh For No Reason, Dora* (Unicorn Theatre); *Let's Build*; *Ready Steady Go, Chocolate Cake, The Borrowers, Under The Rainbow* (Polka Theatre); *Victoria: A Royal Childhood* exhibition (Historic Royal Palaces); *Muckers* (Caroline Horton & The Egg); *Beasty Baby, Big Up!* (TheatreRites); *Lasagna, Sugar, Don't Forget The Birds* (Open Clasp); *No Future* (Adam Welsh & Camden People's Theatre); *Ballad of Maria Marten* (Eastern Angles); *Nothing Happens Twice* (Little Soldier); *The Forum, *untitled, Youthquake, What Once Was Ours* (Zest Theatre); *The Tailor of Gloucester* (Salisbury Playhouse); *How To Win Against History* (Young Vic & Aine Flanagan).

DRUMMOND ORR | Lighting Designer/Production Manager

Drummond has over 40 years' experience as a theatre electrician, technical manager, lighting designer and production manager. In that time, he has toured nationally and internationally, and has worked in both touring and production theatre.

Lighting design credits include: *The Cold Buffet*, *Love It If We Beat Them*, *One Off* (Live Theatre); *The Red Lion* (Live Theatre/Trafalgar Studios); *My Romantic History*, *The Savage*, *Cooking With Elvis* and *Wet House* (Live Theatre/Hull Truck/Soho Theatre); *Tyne*, *The Prize*, *Nativities*, *Two Pints* and *A Walk On Part* (Live Theatre/Soho Theatre/Arts Theatre); *Blackbird* (Market Theatre, Johannesburg); *The Girl in the Yellow Dress* (Market Theatre, Johannesburg/Grahamstown Festival/Baxter Theatre, Cape Town/Citizens, Glasgow); *Educating Rita* (Theatre by the Lake/David Pugh and UK tour).

MATTHEW TUCKEY | Sound Designer

Matthew is a sound designer and sound artist working across theatre, music, installation, podcast and film.

His recent work as sound designer includes: *The Queen of the North* (The Queer Historian at ARC Stockton); *Colliery Boys* R&D (for Harry Rundle at Laurels); *Festen* (Royal Central School of Speech and Drama); *Our Karen – Rainy Days and Mondays* R&D (for David Tuffnell at ARC Stockton); *Love It If We Beat Them* (Live Theatre in association with Emmerson & Ward); *The Sorcerer's Apprentice* (Northern Stage); *Josey* R&D, *Repeat Signal, Lost Found and Told: New Tales for Northumberland* (November Club); *World's Apart, Roaming River* (Woven Nest Theatre); *Wolf!* (Kitchen Zoo in association with Northern Stage); *joey* (gobscure in association with Greyscale Theatre); *Smoke & Mirrors* (Molly Barrett for Enchanted Parks Gateshead); *Floorboards, Trolley Boy, Walter* (Alphabetti Theatre).

His work as sound artist includes: *The Rime* (multichannel immersive installation); *An Audio Diary in Binaural, January 2021* (digital piece for headphones); *South Bend (05-06/20)* (digital EP); *Fed Up, Foodbank Histories Project* (digital piece for headphones for Newcastle University Oral History Unit & Collective).

His work as Associate Sound Designer includes: *Under The Sea* (Tiny Dragon Productions); *You Heard Me* (Luca Rutherford); *When the World is Loud* (Mortal Fools); *A Christmas Carol* (Northern Stage); *Oh No, George!* (Can't Sit Still); *Stella* (Filskit Theatre); *Land: Beating the Bounds* (Northumbria University at Live Theatre).

VERITY NAUGHTON CDG | Casting Director (Royal Court for role of Boy)

Most recent work includes Co-Casting Director on *King & Conqueror* (CBS), young persons' casting on *The Hills of California* and children's casting on *Oliver!* (Chichester Festival Theatre/West End).

Other work includes: UK Casting on *The Hunger Games: The Ballad of Songbirds and Snakes*. As an Associate Casting Director credits include: *The Beautiful Game* (Netflix); *The Book of Clarence* (Legendary); *HALO* (Paramount +); *All the Old Knives* (Amazon); *The First Lady* (Showtime, Lionsgate); *Stephen* (Hat Trick, ITV); *Riviera* (Archery Pictures); *Berlin Station* (Anonymous Content); *Fate: The Winx Saga* (Netflix).

In theatre Verity has cast projects for The Globe, the Royal Court, Southwark Playhouse, Chichester Festival Theatre, and the Almeida Theatre. Having originally specialised in young persons' casting, Verity has cast children in a wealth of West End shows and on screen including: *Enola Holmes* (Netflix); *The Pursuit of Love* (BBC); *Mrs Doubtfire The Musical* (Shaftesbury Theatre); *Frozen The Musical* (Theatre Royal Drury Lane); *Sound of Music* (Chichester Festival Theatre); *Leopoldstadt* (Wyndham's Theatre); *Medea* (Soho Palace Theatre); *Small Island* (National Theatre); *The Ferryman* (Royal Court and Gielgud Theatre); *School of Rock* (UK & international tour); *Beauty & The Beast* (UK tour).

About Live Theatre

'One of the most fertile crucibles of new writing' **The Guardian**

Our vision is for a North East that writes its own story and fights for a more creative future.

Live Theatre occupies a unique place as one of the country's only dedicated new writing buildings outside of London. Across its fifty one-year history it has launched the careers of many of today's leading theatre figures and continues to develop and platform the artists of tomorrow, from playwrights to local school children. Deeply connected to its region and unafraid to confront the most pressing issues of our time, Live Theatre brings ambitious regional artists and adventurous local audiences into vivid contact.

Our mission is to unearth the rich and unexpected narratives of our region, to nurture creativity and bring passionate ideas to life and to be a space that unites people and ignites imaginations.

'Live Theatre has supported generation after generation of new writers, actors and theatre artists.' **Lee Hall, Playwright**

To learn more about Live Theatre and get involved see **www.live.org.uk**

BEST FRIENDS

Noreen Bates
Jim Beirne
Michael and Pat Brown
George Caulkin
Helen Coyne
Lynda and Mike Dillon
Christine Elton
Chris Foy
Robson Green
Brenna Hobson
John Jordan
Graham Maddick
Elaine Orrick
Paul Shevlin
Margaret and
    John Shipley
Shelagh Stephenson
Sting
Alan Tailford
David Walton
Susan Wear
Sue Wilson
Lucy Winskell

GOOD FRIENDS

Vincent Allen
John Appleton
Zoe Blakemore
Jeff Brown
Alec Collerton
Chris Connell
    and Lucy Nichol
Ron Cook
Joe Douglas
Ross Freeman
Ann Gittins
Eileen Jones
Richard Kain
John Mason
Rhys McKinnell
Linda Norris
Michelle Percy

Pat Ritchie
Martin Saunders
Phil Skingley
Susan and Mike Stewart
John Stokel-Walker
John Tomaney
Angela Walton
K F Walton
Mary and Steve Wootten

FRIENDS

Pat Allcorn
Sharon Austin
Norma Banfi
Simon Barker
Bex Bowsher
Lynn Boyes
Lawrence Bryson
Rob Chapman
Angela Cooper
Sally-Anne Cooper
Judy Cowgill
Glynis Downie
Suky Drummond
Keith Elliott
Sue Emmas
Robert Fairfax
Carolyn Ford
John Graham
Julie Grant
Moira Gray
Norma Harris
Gael Henry
Ruth and Robert Heyman
Gillian Hitchenes
Wendy Holland
Irene Hudson
Beverley Jewitt
Nicole Kavanagh-Stubbs
John Loughlin
Gen Lowes
Stephanie Malyon
Michael McBride

Ian McPherson
Catherine Moody
Linda Moss
David Nellist
Michael Nielsen
Jean Ollerton
Mark Olney
Clare Overton
Jonathan Pye
David Robertson
Jo Robinson
Julian Rogan
Jean Scott
Jill Scrimshaw
Alan and Rosalind Share
Monica Shaw
Jo Shepherd
Ian and Christine
    Shepherdson
Tracey Sinclair
David Slater
Brent Taylorson
Don Tennet
Robert Vardill
Sandra Wake
Jennifer Wallace
Sue Ward
Heather Wilkinson
Keith Williamson

Plus those who choose to
remain anonymous

Live Theatre Staff

Executive Director/Joint Chief Executive	Jacqui Kell
Artistic Director/Joint Chief Executive	Jack McNamara
PA to Joint Chief Executives	Alex Readman

Creative Programme

New Work Producer	JD Stewart
Artist Development Producer	John Dawson
Associate Artists	gobscure
	Kemi-Bo Jacobs

Children and Young People

CYPP Leader	Helen Green
Senior Creative Associate CYPP	Paul James
CYPP Administrator	Amy Foley
Creative Lead Live Tales	Becky Morris

Technical Production

Production Manager	Drummond Orr
Technical and Digital Manager	David Flynn
Technician	Taylor Howie
Estates and Maintenance Assistant	Ken Evans

Operations and Finance

Finance Manager	Antony Robertson
Finance and Payroll Officer	Catherine Moody
Fundraising and Development Manager	Alison Nicholson

Marketing and Communications

Marketing and Communications Manager	Lisa Campbell
Marketing and Communications Manager	Michele McCallion
Marketing and Communications Officer	Arthur Roberts

Customer Services and Box Office

Duty Manager	Michael Davies
Duty Manager and Bar Supervisor	Alicia Meehan
Duty Manager and Bar Supervisor	Sarah Matthews
Duty Manager and Bar Supervisor	Patrycja Nowacka
Duty Manager and Bar Supervisor	Jake Wilson Craw
Bar Supervisor	Fay Carrington
Customer Services Assistant	Elisha Ewing
Customer Services Assistant	Caitlin Fairlamb
Customer Services Assistant	Elspeth Frith
Customer Services Assistant	Joel Houghton
Customer Services Assistant	Lukas Gabryseh
Customer Services Assistant	Alicja Gadomski
Customer Services Assistant	Joe Kell
Customer Services Assistant	Kathryn Watt

Box Office Assistant	Daniel Ball
Box Office Assistant	Asa Beckett
Box Office Assistant	Steven Blackshaw
Box Office Assistant	Joseph Duffy
Box Office Assistant	Ruby Taylor
Box Office Assistant	Jasper Wilding

Housekeeping

Housekeeping	Lydia Igbinosa
Housekeeping	Jean Kent
Housekeeping	Angela Salem
Housekeeping	Camille Vitorino-Itoua

THE ROYAL COURT THEATRE

The Royal Court Theatre is the writers' theatre. It is a leading force in world theatre for cultivating and supporting writers - undiscovered, emerging and established.

Since 1956, we have commissioned and produced hundreds of writers, from John Osborne to Mohamed-Zain Dada. Royal Court plays from every decade are now performed on stages and taught in classrooms and universities across the globe.

Through the writers, the Royal Court is at the forefront of creating restless, alert, provocative theatre about now. We open our doors to the unheard voices and free thinkers that, through their writing, change our way of seeing.

We strive to create an environment in which differing voices and opinions can co-exist. In current times, it is becoming increasingly difficult for writers to write what they want or need to write without fear, and we will do everything we can to rise above a narrowing of viewpoints.

Through all our work, we strive to inspire audiences and influence future writers with radical thinking and provocative discussion.

🐦 royalcourt 🅵 royalcourttheatre

ARTS COUNCIL ENGLAND
Supported using public funding by

ROYAL COURT SUPPORTERS

Our incredible community of supporters makes it possible for us to achieve our mission of nurturing and platforming writers at every stage of their careers. Our supporters are part of our essential fabric – they help to give us the freedom to take bigger and bolder risks in our work, develop and empower new voices, and create world-class theatre that challenges and disrupts the theatre ecology.

To all our supporters, thank you. You help us to write the future.

PUBLIC FUNDING

CHARITABLE PARTNERS

BackstageTrust

T. S. ELIOT FOUNDATION

JERWOOD
FOUNDATION

CORPORATE SPONSORS
Aqua Financial Ltd
Cadogan
Edwardian Hotels, London
Sustainable Wine Solutions

SIS
TER

CORPORATE MEMBERS
Bloomberg Philanthropies
Sloane Stanley

TRUSTS AND FOUNDATIONS
Maria Björnson Memorial Fund
Martin Bowley Charitable Trust
Chalk Cliff Trust
The Noël Coward Foundation
Cowley Charitable Foundation
The Davidson Play GC Bursary
The Lynne Gagliano Writer's Award
The Golden Bottle Trust
The Harold Hyam Wingate Foundation
John Lyon's Charity
The Marlow Trust
Clare McIntyre's Bursary
Old Possum's Practical Trust
The Austin & Hope Pilkington Trust
Richard Radcliffe Charitable Trust
Rose Foundation
Royal Victoria Hall Foundation
The Thistle Trust
The Thompson Family Charitable Trust

INDIVIDUAL SUPPORTERS

Artistic Director's Circle

Katie Bradford
Jeremy & Becky Broome
Clyde Cooper
Debbie De Girolamo &
Ben Babcock
Dominique & Neal Gandhi
Lydia & Manfred Gorvy
David & Jean Grier
Charles Holloway
Linda Keenan
Andrew & Ariana Rodger
Jack Thorne & Rachel Mason
Anonymous

Writers' Circle

Chris & Alison Cabot
Robyn Durie
Mr & Mrs Duncan Matthews KC
Emma O'Donoghue
Maureen & Tony Wheeler
Anonymous

Directors' Circle

Piers Butler
Fiona Clements
Professor John Collinge
Julian & Ana Garel-Jones
Carol Hall
Dr Timothy Hyde
Anonymous

Platinum Members

Moira Andreae
Tyler Bollier
Katie Bullivant
Anthony Burton CBE
Matthew Dean
Sally & Giles Everist
Emily Fletcher
Beverley Gee
Damien Hyland
Susanne Kapoor
David P Kaskel & Christopher
A Teano
Peter & Maria Kellner
Robert Ledger & Sally
 Moulsdale
Frances Lynn
Mrs Janet Martin
Andrew McIver
Andrea & Hilary Ponti
Corinne Rooney
Anita Scott
Bhags Sharma
Dr Wendy Sigle
Brian Smith
Mrs Caroline Thomas
Sir Robert & Lady Wilson
Anonymous

With thanks to our Silver and Gold Supporters, and our Friends and Good Friends, whose support we greatly appreciate.

LET'S BE FRIENDS. WITH BENEFITS.

Our Friends and Good Friends are part of the fabric of the Royal Court. They help us to create world-class theatre, and in return they receive early access to our shows and a range of exclusive benefits.

Join today and become a part of our community.

BECOME A FRIEND
From £40 a year

Benefits include:

- Priority Booking
- Advanced access to £15 Monday tickets
- 10% discount in our Bar & Kitchen (including Court in the Square) and Samuel French bookshop

BECOME A GOOD FRIEND
From £95 a year

In addition to the Friend benefits, our Good Friends also receive:

- Five complimentary playtexts for Royal Court productions
- An invitation for two to step behind the scenes of the Royal Court Theatre at a special event

Our Good Friends' membership also includes a voluntary donation.
This extra support goes directly towards supporting our work and future, both on and off stage.

To become a Friend or a Good Friend, or to find out more about the different ways in which you can get involved, visit our website: royalcourttheatre.com/support-us

The English Stage Company at the Royal Court Theatre is a registered charity (No. 231242)

THE BOUNDS

Stewart Pringle

Acknowledgements

Thanks to everyone who's befriended this play on its long, strange trip. Firstly to Jack, a spectacular director who I have admired for years, and also the man who said 'let's do it' – the finest gift a playwright can be given – and to JD and the whole excellent team at Live Theatre for making this happen. To David, Will, Gill and all at the Royal Court for bringing the Allen Valleys to Sloane Square, it's such a privilege to be in the first season of artists and humans I love and respect so much. To the outrageously talented team who are bringing this show to life: to Verity, Matthew, Drummond, Jayne, Lou, Craig and Taylor. To our incredible cast: Ryan, Lauren, and Soroosh; to James, Nathaniel, Harry, Wilbur and all their chaperones and families.

To my wonderful agent Jonathan, for his constant support and friendship, who took me to Loftus Road to learn the true meaning of unconditional love. And to his parents Tom and Janie, who put me up in Journey's End and fed me lobster bisque and G&Ts while the plays got written in the Budleigh sun. To lovely, wise Matt at Nick Hern Books, who has read countless unproduced plays of mine and never told me to sod off, and to Sarah Liisa, Deborah, Maddie, Nick and the whole NHB team – caring publishers who are still finding new village halls for Harry and Denise to put a table up in.

To Tudor football expert Professor Steven Gunn of Merton College, Oxford, for his early help with the research, which was so valuable in sharpening and widening the play's scope and interests. All historical inaccuracies are, of course, entirely my own. And to the Tudor House, Margate, for kicking this all off.

Apologies to Norwich City FC and Henry VIII for plagiarising your lyrics for the ancient Dales' chant.

Thanks for the early enthusiasm and support from Clive Judd, Barney Norris and Tim Foley. To Andy Routledge for all his kindness and efforts on the play's behalf, I hope we can work together soon. To the Peggy Ramsay Foundation, who have bailed me out of penury more than once. To the Papatango boys for giving me the confidence to keep going at such a crucial moment.

To Nina, Rachel, Sasha, Ola, Jessy, Rufus, Clint and everyone else at the National Theatre who have given me the time, space and belief to make this show.

To Samuel, Liam, Tom, Heather, Alice and too many other pals to mention for thousands of pints and decades of friendship and support. To all the Hot Bobs for keeping me sane, and everyone at Big Finish for keeping me writing.

To Mike Fry, always, whose memory and legacy of passion drives me every day.

Endless love and thanks to my family, to my outrageously wonderful sisters Heather and Iona, and to Mum and Dad, who have always kept a light burning on the side of the valley, so I can find my way home. Particular thanks to my beloved Uncle Cecil, who passed away during the writing of this play, who was as gentle and supportive as anyone I've ever known, and whose knowledge of Allendale was as deep and mysterious as the drop shafts on Carr Shield fell. I wish you were here.

And finally to my beautiful, brave, and brilliant wife Lauren, who sees the world so clearly, and loves it anyway. For all the love, support, and the little trips. Thank you.

S.P.

To Mum & Dad

Characters

PERCY, *twenty-two years old*
ROWAN, *twenty-six years old*
SAMUEL, *twenty-one years old*
BOY, *eight years old*

Setting

A muddy patch of Northumbrian earth in the mid-sixteenth century.

It's Whitsuntide.

Note on Text

A forward slash (/) indicates the next line is to interrupt the current one.

Words in [square brackets] are unspoken or almost spoken.

Line breaks in the text denote a pause or silence.

The presence or absence of punctuation should give some idea of rhythm and the completeness or otherwise of thoughts and speech.

This text went to press before the end of rehearsals and so may differ slightly from the play as performed.

The First Day

PERCY *stands in the first light of dawn. He's dressed for a football match. He's covered in mud, but then he always is. He checks his tunic and his shoes, finds his footing, coughs, puts his hands behind his back, and he sings.*

As he sings, the sun rises weakly in a cold spring sky.

PERCY   Pastime with good company
I love and shall until I die;
Complain who will, but none deny
If God be pleased then so shall I.

In days to come, when come and gone
Our boyhood's game of friends
When our youthful vigour has declined
Into our lonesome ends.

You'll think on times, those happy times
Their memories fond recall
When in the bloom of youthful prime
We kept upon the ball.

Kick it off, throw it in, have a little scrimmage
Keep it low, splendid rush, bravo, win or die;
On the ball, Allendale, never mind the danger,
Steady on, now's your chance,
God's heart! We've scored a goal!

ROWAN *enters and watches from a distance.*
She wears a rough dress and a scarf. She's covered in mud too.

Let all tonight then drink with me
To the football game we love,
And wish it may successful be
As other games of old,
And in one grand united toast

> Join player, game and song
> And fondly pledge your pride and toast
> Success to all the 'Dale.

PERCY/ROWAN   Kick it off –

PERCY   Alright.

PERCY/ROWAN   Throw in, have a little scrimmage,
Keep it low, splendid rush, bravo, win or die;
On the ball, Allendale, never mind the danger,
Steady on, now's your chance,
God's heart! We've scored a goal!

PERCY steps forwards and claps, loud and slow.

PERCY   That's what I'm talking about.
That is what I'm talking about.

ROWAN   Don't.

ROWAN is standing, tensed and frozen, eyes closed.

PERCY   That is / what I'm

ROWAN   Percy –

PERCY   What's that?

ROWAN   I said don't so don't, alright?
Just let me have this.

Pause.

PERCY   Let you have what?

ROWAN   This.

PERCY   This / what?

ROWAN   Can you just?

PERCY   Course.

Beat.

But what is – ?

ROWAN *bursts out of it*.

ROWAN   Oh forget it.
          Forget it!

PERCY   Well, I didn't know what you were doing!

ROWAN   I was just trying to appreciate it.
          You should try it as well.

PERCY   Appreciate what?

ROWAN   This bit.
          Match-day morning.
          First light.
          Just before the bells.

PERCY   What?

ROWAN   Just do it!

          ROWAN *goes back into her trance*. PERCY
          follows.

          Smell the grass.

          They do.

          That's it.
          All across the valley,
          The sun's coming up.
          It's a brand-new day.
          It's the day.

PERCY   It's the day.

ROWAN   And everything's fine.

PERCY   Everything's fine.

ROWAN   Everything's good.

PERCY   Everything's good.

ROWAN   Everything's just perfect.
          Because right now, in this perfect frozen moment
          We haven't fucked it up yet.

PERCY   Now, hang on –

           PERCY *breaks out of it.* ROWAN *still entranced.*

ROWAN   It's all still to play for.
           God hasn't played his hand yet.

           We haven't had our dicks kicked halfway to Carr
           Shield fell by Catton yet.
           We haven't had our great white hope arse-fucked,
           tarred, feathered, drawn, quartered, privies roasted,
           arse-fucked again and then invalided off the pitch
           by Catton.
           Not yet we haven't!
           Not yet!

           We should treasure this, Perce.
           We should treasure it.
           Because right now, right this minute
           WE ARE CHAMPIONS!

           ROWAN *raises her arms and breathes in deeply.*

           Pause.

PERCY   What
           What a bloody

           What an
           Attitude
           What a bloody attitude to have
           I'm, fucking
           I'm speechless.

ROWAN   Kings of the world!
           (*Singing.*) God's heart! We've scored a go–

           Ah, no.
           It's passing, it's passing.

           ROWAN *exhales, opens her eyes.*

           It's passed.

           ROWAN *claps* PERCY *on the shoulder, shakes
           herself down, spits.*

Come on, then.
Let's get reamed by some farmers!

PERCY   Why are you like this?

ROWAN   Like what?
Like realistic?

PERCY   No?

ROWAN   Sort of grounded?

Sort of realistic, grounded
Like sort of a rational grounded sort of realist
Sort of like that?

PERCY   Like a prick.

ROWAN   Experience.
Age, wisdom and experience.

PERCY   Like an old prick then.

ROWAN   I'm just saying
1547

PERCY   Don't start.

ROWAN   Obliterated.
'48?
Trounced.

'49
'49 I actually thought we were in with a shot.
Actually thought we were getting somewhere.
John Brock on green front forward.

PERCY   John Brock!

ROWAN   Badger Brock.
Shithouse stocky.
Cokesegge backing him up by the pump.
Cokesegge who bit through an actual iron manacle
when he was up for outraging himself on
Martinmas.
Crusher Cokesegge!

And not only do we lose in less than half-a-fucking-
hour but John Brock gets a mason jar smashed
through his eye socket and he never plays again.

PERCY   The bastards.

ROWAN   1550's a day-long bloodbath
'51 it rains so hard John Hipper actually drowns
And last year

PERCY   Alright that's enough!
God's sake!

ROWAN   Just saying
Hope for the best
Expect the worst.

PERCY   There's a word for people like you actually.
You're a defeatist.
You don't want us to win, you want us to lose.

ROWAN   Bollocks.

PERCY   You want us to lose because it's more exciting
for you.
You want us to lose so you can sit down Sunday
evening at that long table at the back of The White
Cock and bitch about it with your creepy mate with
blue hands.

ROWAN   Fuck off.

PERCY   And that's God's truth.

ROWAN   Fuck –

PERCY   Mewling
Like a couple of ewes / with tangled guts.

ROWAN   Off.

PERCY   Bleating on.
Bleating on and on with your blue-handed fuck-
ugly mate.
Mehhhhh.
Mehhh-ehhh-ehhh.

ROWAN   You done?

           I don't want us to lose.

PERCY   Sure.

ROWAN   I want us to win.
           I want us to win.
           I do.

           I just don't want you to get your hopes up.

           PERCY *pulls a scarf, dyed in team colours, out of his pocket and wraps it around his neck.*

PERCY   Yeah, well it's a bit late for that.

ROWAN   (*The scarf.*) That new?

PERCY   Yep.

ROWAN   It's nice.

PERCY   Thank you very much.

ROWAN   Rosie weave that for you?

PERCY   Yes.

ROWAN   Oh, she has got it bad.

PERCY   Fuck off.

ROWAN   Wants a slice of that Lamrose mutton.

PERCY   Shut your fucking mouth.

ROWAN   Wants you to whip it out

           Mimes it.

           Ker-boosh.
           Slap it down.
           Slap it right down.

PERCY

ROWAN   And lay it on her.
           Kerrrr-boosh!

PERCY   You're disgusting.
             You disgust me.
             Think you can just say owt, don't you?

ROWAN   I do, yeah.

PERCY   Yeah, well

             PERCY *stamps. Pause.*

             Cold.
             So bloody cold.
             Like a witch's

             Glances at ROWAN, *who grins.*

             Breast.

ROWAN   Least it's clear.
             Ground's hard though.

             ROWAN *kicks the soil.*

PERCY   It'll soften.
             Sun's up.

ROWAN   We're shite when it's hard.

PERCY   There you go again!
             Dragging us down!

ROWAN   Sorry, sorry!
             I just
             After last year I just

PERCY   I don't want to talk about last year.
             I've told you exactly what I thought about last year.
             I've said all I've got to say about last year.
             Alright?
             Let's just listen.

ROWAN   I just

PERCY   Let's just
             Listen, alright.
             I'm not missing the start again.

             Pause.

ROWAN   Was in The Cock last night.

PERCY   You do surprise me.

ROWAN   Want to know what I saw?

PERCY   No, I want to listen.

         What did you see then?

         Pause.

ROWAN   Thomas Lockley.

PERCY

         You're a liar.

ROWAN   God's truth.
         Thomas Lockley.
         Putting them away.

PERCY   He shouldn't be putting anything away.
         Thomas Lockley, you're sure?

ROWAN   Think anyone's getting mistaken for Thomas
         Lockley?

PERCY   He's first forward, he shouldn't be in The Cock on
         match eve.

ROWAN   Joan and Edith there, mouths hanging open like that
         Like cows that've been clobbered.
         Grubby hands up his thighs like a pair of squirrels.

PERCY   His thighs?

ROWAN   Up his massive thighs.

PERCY   So it *was* Thomas Lockley.
         And he was drinking?

         On match eve?

ROWAN   Er, yeah.
         Drinking a lot.

PERCY   The stupid bastard!
         He's supposed to be resting up.

ROWAN   Resting up in Edith Bridkirk from what I saw.

PERCY   Oh! What?
          Edith bloody Bridkirk?

ROWAN   Yep.

PERCY   I'm angry now.
          He's our best forward, he's
          Oh, oh fuck it then.
          Fuck it.
          That's the year
          That's the whole year
          Ruined.
          Ruined!
          That's, that's
          If Thomas Lockley doesn't give a shit about this
          village
          If he wants to use up his vital
          Whatever, / with Edith Bridkirk

ROWAN   Gross.

PERCY   If he's happy for us to get our name dragged
          through the mud by Catton
          By those smug arseholes in Catton
          If he doesn't mind twelve more months of being
          told you play like bloody papists and
          And Philip fucking Bunting pointing at donkeys on
          market day and saying 'That's you that is'
          Or, or shouting 'Oh-ho, here comes the Allendale
          team' when it's just a lot of schoolgirls in dresses
          that he's
          You know
          Indicating
          If he doesn't mind that, any of that!
          Then he can shove his football game up his arse!

          PERCY *takes off his scarf and throws it onto the
          ground. Stamps on it twice.*

ROWAN   Only joking.

PERCY   What?

ROWAN   I was joking.
         It was just a joke.

PERCY   Was it?

ROWAN   Course it was.

         It wasn't.

         Thomas Lockley?
         In The Cock on match eve?
         Nah.
         Not the Tommy-Lockers.
         He's the best front forward we've got.

PERCY   He is.

ROWAN   Exactly.
         You see?
         Joke-ing!

PERCY   Oh!
         Oh you bloody
         Terror.
         You terror.

ROWAN   Had you there.

PERCY   No.

ROWAN   Had you good and proper.

         PERCY *picks up his scarf and brushes it off.*

PERCY   Aye, maybe.
         Maybe just a bit.
         Edith Bridkirk!

ROWAN   Mind you, / I wouldn't put it past –

PERCY   Shh!
         Listen.

         A distant toll of a bell.

ROWAN   That's it.

PERCY   Almost.

The bell tolls six. PERCY *counts. He readies himself.* ROWAN *gets into position a few feet away.*

Three, come on
Four
Five, get ready
Six
Six!
It is on and we are off!

(*Roaring.*) COME ON THEN!

Silence.

COME ON THEN!

PERCY *slaps himself on the face, the thighs, finds his footing, hunkers down.*

Silence.

PERCY *spits.*

Silence.

COME ON / THEN!

ROWAN   Alright, Perce.

PERCY   Sorry.

Silence.

Can you, erm
You
You see / anything?

ROWAN   Nope.

PERCY *squints. Shields the sun from his eyes. Stands on tiptoes.*

PERCY   They want to chop those trees down.
It's all behind the
They've got ridiculous.

Whose
Whose trees do you reckon they are?

ROWAN   No clue.

PERCY *squints*.

PERCY   Some
Tree
Wanker.

Silence.

Is that Thomas?

ROWAN   You what?

PERCY   It is!
THOMAS!
GIVE THEM HELL, THOMAS!
FUCK THEM UP, THE CATTON BASTARDS!

(*Singing.*) Catton, Catton you are shit!
Catton you are full of it!

PERCY *roars*.

God's fucking blood!
That's Thomas!
THOMAS!
THOMAS?

ROWAN   Is it Thomas?

PERCY   Yes!

I think so.

Pause.

Thomas is just
(*Growls.*)
Isn't he?
He's just – ah!
Thomas.

ROWAN   Aye.

           ROWAN *spits. Surveys the pitch.*

           Listen, don't take this the wrong way.
           You sure this is where he said?

PERCY   What?

ROWAN   You sure this is where he said to be?
           John.

PERCY   Course I am.
           He said level with Woolly Burn and the tree that
           looks like a bear doing a big long punch.

           Poses.

ROWAN   Right.

PERCY   Why's that?

ROWAN   No reason.

           It's just.
           I think it's, I think we're, we are

           Further away than last year.

PERCY   No, it's
           Last year we were right by mine which is over
           Well it's

           Indicates to the right.

           It's

           Indicates to the right.

           Isn't it?
           So I can see why you might think
           I can see why it seems further but actually
           Actually

ROWAN   It is further.
           It's much further.

PERCY   Ah but further from where?
           Because the starting line is

Indicates ahead of them.

And Catton goal is

Indicates to the right and behind them.

So

ROWAN   So however you measure it, we're further out,
aren't we?

PERCY   Nah
I'd say we're slightly, ever so slightly closer.
Anyway it's tactics.
John's tactics.
We're rear defence.
We're always backward rear defence.
Always.
And if it looks further away to you, that's just the
lie of the land.
That's just your eyes playing tricks on you.
We're the closest we've ever been.
They say we're on the outside, but really
Really we're right in the middle.
Right in the middle of the action.

Pause.

ROWAN   Yeah, sod this.

ROWAN *goes to leave.*

PERCY   What are you
What you doing?

ROWAN   I'm moving.

PERCY   You're what?

ROWAN   I'm moving.
I'm moving forward.
This is shite, Perce.

PERCY   But you can't move.

ROWAN   Can't I.

ROWAN *takes a few steps forwards.*

PERCY   You get back here.
        You get back here right now.

ROWAN   Make me.

PERCY   I will.

ROWAN   Go on then.

        PERCY *makes a tentative step over.*

        You lay one finger on me and I'll put you on your
        arse Percy Lamrose.

PERCY   Come back here then!
        John said / we're to

ROWAN   Oh John said, did he?
        John said?
        Master tactician John fucking Ridley.
        Squiddly Ridley.
        Only reason he's the bloody captain is he'd have
        his drunk baldy little head flattened like windfall if
        he actually played the game.
        Because he knows he'd shite it in the first five
        minutes.

PERCY   He's just had a bad run.

ROWAN   Oh yeah.

PERCY   Needs time to find his feet.
        He's got a plan.
        We've to stick to his plan.

ROWAN   Look, Percy
        Maybe he does
        Maybe he does have a plan
        I just don't know how much difference it's going to
        make to anything
        To any of it
        If his two pig-shittest, clod-footed fucking
        liabilities of defenders move five hundred yards

down the valley so they can actually see some of the game.
You get me?

PERCY *is stung.*

PERCY   You take that back.

ROWAN   You what?

PERCY   We're here because this is where John needs us.
It's tactical.

ROWAN   It's doltish.

PERCY   We're backward rear defenders!

ROWAN   We're barely even fucking spectators!
If we were any further away we'd be in the next county.

PERCY   We're marking the pitch edge, in case

ROWAN   In case what?

PERCY   In case

ROWAN   In case?
There's nothing to defend.
There's nobody to mark.
There's nobody here for
FUCKING
MILES!

SAMUEL *has approached them, unseen. His clothes are clean, and bright.*

SAMUEL   She's right actually

PERCY *grabs* ROWAN *and pulls her back into position.*

Apart from me, obviously, I'm here.
But apart from me there's nobody for miles.
It's quite peaceful, really.
I've been up for ages, walking.

> There was hoar frost earlier, did you see it?
> In June! Imagine that!
> God's breath.
>
> Hello.

PERCY   Hands in the air!

SAMUEL   Excuse me?

PERCY   Put your fucking hands where I can see them!

ROWAN   Why?

SAMUEL   Yes, why?

PERCY   Just put your hands in the air, alright?

SAMUEL   Alright.

> *He does.*

ROWAN   What you on?

> PERCY *approaches* SAMUEL *and pats him down.*
>
> Percy?

SAMUEL   I'm not armed.

PERCY   Oh yeah.

> *Finished.*
>
> Could have had the ball secreted about his person.
> Sneak it through enemy lines.

SAMUEL   Where?

ROWAN   Really?

PERCY   Could be a spy.

ROWAN   A spy.

SAMUEL   I'm not a spy.

PERCY   Could be from Catton.

SAMUEL   I'm not from Catton.

PERCY   He's got a witchy look to him, hasn't he?

SAMUEL   A what?

PERCY   Wouldn't you say, Ro?

ROWAN   No.

PERCY   I think he has.
            Right witchy Catton-y look to him this one.
            Looks like a pervert.

SAMUEL   I don't know what you're talking about.

ROWAN   Yeah, neither do I to be honest.

PERCY   They mess about with witches in Catton.
            The men do.

ROWAN   Bollocks do they.

PERCY   Absolutely they do.
            Lads from Catton.
            Proven witch-fiddlers.

ROWAN   What proof could you possibly have?

PERCY   You know Gerald?

ROWAN   Gerald the Mad Miller?

PERCY   That's him.

ROWAN   So?

PERCY   So he got gobbed off by a witch.

ROWAN   He did not.

PERCY   And when he woke up next morning someone had
            mended his mill wheel but his tadger'd gone black
            as tar.

ROWAN   Where do you get this / from?

SAMUEL   I am not from Catton.

PERCY   Well where are you from, then?
            I've not seen you before.

SAMUEL   I've seen you.

PERCY
             Well I find that very suspicious.
             I find it suspicious.
             And weird.
             And just like very, deeply
             Very suspicious.
             And –

ROWAN   I've seen him.

PERCY   Have you?

ROWAN   Yeah I have.
             He's Allendale.

SAMUEL   I really am.

PERCY   Which part?

SAMUEL   East.

PERCY   East?

SAMUEL   That's right.
             Where are you?

PERCY   Well I'm west.

ROWAN   There you go then.

PERCY   You know him?

ROWAN   I know his father.

PERCY   You know his father?

ROWAN   God's sake, Perce, pack it in
             I know his father, his father's –

SAMUEL   Nicholas Jaane.

ROWAN   Right.

PERCY   Nick Jaane?

SAMUEL   That's right.

PERCY   But I thought Nick Jaane was

Gestures vaguely to his crotch.

ROWAN   Nope.

PERCY   Nick Jaane.
         But he's loaded isn't he?

SAMUEL   If you say so.

PERCY   He lives in a
         I mean, he's properly loaded.

SAMUEL   He's a farmer.

PERCY   He's a squire.

SAMUEL   He is.

PERCY   So where've you been?

ROWAN   He's been away.

PERCY   He's been what?

SAMUEL   My father sent me away.
         I've been away for years.
         It's quite common with the sons of
         It's quite common.

PERCY   Where'd he send you?

SAMUEL   Oxford.

PERCY   Fuck.
         (*Spits.*)
         Full of twats.

SAMUEL   Have you been?

PERCY   No I haven't been.
         I obviously haven't been.
         What, you think there's a sort of grand cultural tour
         we get sent on?
         My da, my fucking 'father'
         My da had about seven sheep the whole time I was

growing up and two of those drowned in Talking
Tarn because they were so

Thick

So no
I never did quite make it down, pip fucking pip.
But I've heard about it.
Heard plenty.

PERCY *stomps away.*

ROWAN   We don't get out of the valley much.

PERCY   Errm, we don't want to get out of the valley much!
Fucking Oxford.

SAMUEL   Alright.

PERCY   So what's a clergyman doing in the middle of the
game, then?
This isn't for squires, or squires' sons.

SAMUEL   Is it not?

PERCY   No.

SAMUEL   Why not?

PERCY   Because it just isn't.
It's dangerous.

SAMUEL   Doesn't look very dangerous.

PERCY   Well it is.
People die playing the game.

SAMUEL   Die?

PERCY   Often.

ROWAN   Not often.

PERCY   Often enough!
Often enough if you're the one who gets his nose,
like, squished into his brain and dies.
Often enough if you're him!

ROWAN   Or John Hipper.

PERCY   Or John Hipper!
            He drowned in 1551!
            Drowned on dry land.

SAMUEL   Golly.

PERCY   Golly?

SAMUEL   Poor John.

PERCY   Yes!
            Yes poor John, you're right.
            Poor fucking John Hipper.
            So it's not the place for any milk-sopping,
            cap-wearing, silver-spoon-having-up-his-arse-ing,
            Oxford-going, squire's son cunt, thank you
            very much.
            So bugger off.

            Pause.

SAMUEL   Right.
            See you later then.

            SAMUEL *moves away, not very far away, and
            stands.*

            Pause.

PERCY   What are you doing?

SAMUEL   Just taking the air.

PERCY   What are you doing standing there, I mean?
            You're supposed to have buggered off.

SAMUEL   I have.

PERCY   You have –
            You have not.
            You haven't buggered –
            You're still here.

SAMUEL   Depends how you look at it.

PERCY *gestures to* ROWAN, *furious*.

ROWAN   I'm staying out of it.
          He can stand where he likes for all I care.

SAMUEL   Thank you!

PERCY   Ah ah ah!
          Don't you talk to her.
          Don't you talk to her, she's playing the game.
          The ball's in play.

SAMUEL   Right, sorry.

PERCY   'Sake.
          And get off the pitch!

SAMUEL   I thought I had.

PERCY   You what?

SAMUEL   I thought I'd
          Well, where does the pitch end, exactly?

PERCY   I'm not telling you.

SAMUEL   Right.

PERCY   You shouldn't even be talking to me.
          Bugger off the sodding pitch, alright?

SAMUEL   But how will I know?

PERCY   Know what?

SAMUEL   How will I know whether I'm on the pitch or not if
          you don't tell me where it ends?
          There aren't any flags.

PERCY   Flags?
          Flags?
          It's not a fucking nancy Oxford fucking la-di-di
          whatever.
          It's the football.
          It's the game.
          Flags are for papists and perverts.

Never trust a man who spends too much time
with flags.
Flags are, at best, women's business.
At best!
No offence, Rowan.

ROWAN   I mean, none taken.

SAMUEL   The copse over there.
Is that copse on the pitch?

PERCY   Yes.

SAMUEL   Right.
And the riverbank.

PERCY   Obviously.

SAMUEL   And the whole village / area

PERCY   Is the absolute dead-centre middle of the fucking
pitch, yes.

ROWAN   It's a big pitch.

SAMUEL   You can say that again.

ROWAN   Right, so
You know Splitty Lane, upwards of Catton.

SAMUEL   Yes.

ROWAN   That's the boundary line to the north.
Thornley Gate marks the east.
Crook of the Allen, that's the south.

PERCY   And the west boundary you're standing on.
Parallel with Woolly Burn and just east of my
place.

SAMUEL   Wow.

PERCY   It's big.

ROWAN   It's four miles across at the widest part.

SAMUEL   Wow.

PERCY   Yes wow.

SAMUEL   So why are you so far away then?

            Sharp intakes of breath.

PERCY   You what?

SAMUEL   I just wondered why you're
            You know
            Why you're both so far away from the middle.

PERCY   Know a lot about football do you?

SAMUEL   No, I

PERCY   So shut your face then.
            It's tactics.

ROWAN   And we're a bit shit.

PERCY   Ey ey ey!
            Enough from you!

SAMUEL   So what do you do?

PERCY   You play the game.

SAMUEL   Right.
            So is it like stoolball or

PERCY   Is it like?
            Fucking

ROWAN   Steady on.

PERCY   I'm going to punch him.
            If I wasn't
            If I wasn't playing an integral part in the most
            important
            The most important game
            Possibly of our lives
            If I wasn't disciplined
            Focused
            Primed for victory
            I would put my fist through your face for that.

               Fucking
               Stoolball!

SAMUEL   What's wrong with stoolball?

PERCY   Oh, let me see now, let me think
               Only that it's totally shit!

ROWAN   Good one.

PERCY   That what they play in Oxford is it?
               Load of men in ruffs slapping each other's arses
               with sticks.
               That's what passes for a good time in Oxford is it?
               Stoolball.

SAMUEL   They might play it in Oxford.
               I watched them play it in Sussex.

ROWAN   Oh yeah.

SAMUEL   In Rye.
               Stoolball's very popular in Sussex.

ROWAN   So I hear.

SAMUEL   What do you mean?

ROWAN   Got a fancy girl you've got your eye on?

SAMUEL   What? No!

ROWAN   Yeah yeah.
               Bit of Sussex skirt, is it?
               Bit of tinkering down in Rye?

SAMUEL   I don't know what you
               I just like the game.

ROWAN   Nobody likes stoolball.

PERCY   That's right.

ROWAN   They watch it for the totty.
               Flash of some milkmaid's scabby knees.

SAMUEL   No.

ROWAN   All those silk-white hands on stiff Sussex bats!

SAMUEL   That's enough!

ROWAN   I see you.

Satisfied. SAMUEL *reddening.*

PERCY   They've got women playing stoolball?

ROWAN   Course they have.
          They love it down there in Sussex.

SAMUEL   Don't women play the game?

PERCY   The game?
          Fuck no.
          Apart from Rowan.

SAM   Why's that?

ROWAN   I'm the exception that proves the rule.

PERCY   It's dangerous.
          I've told you.

SAMUEL   So what do you do?

PERCY   You what?

SAMUEL   What are the rules?

ROWAN   Shall I?

PERCY *gestures 'whatever'.*

Strike of six, Friday of Whitsuntide weekend.

SAMUEL   Today.

ROWAN   Today.
          So.
          Ball's pitched.
          You know pitched?

SAMUEL   Thrown?

ROWAN   Yes, sort of.
          Tossed, really.

Ball's tossed in Mill Yard.
That's precisely halfway between Allendale and Catton.
Then there's two posts.

SAMUEL   Right.

ROWAN   Two posts in the village squares.

PERCY   One a-piece.

ROWAN   And there's usually, what, forty or fifty players a side?
That's most every lad in the village, unless he's lame.

PERCY   Mind you some of the lame ones are quite handy.

ROWAN   You're village green forward, mid-forward or rear forward.
Those are the attackers, they try to get the ball to the opposing green.
Then there's the front defence, mid-defence and rear defence.

PERCY   And backward rear defence.

ROWAN   Right.
And they try to keep the ball away from their own green, you see?

SAMUEL   I see.

ROWAN   Second it touches either post, the game's over.

PERCY   Game over.

SAMUEL   And that's it?

ROWAN   Simple as.

SAMUEL   How long does a match last?

ROWAN   It lasts until it's done.
Could be a few hours. Could be a day.
Could be more.

PERCY   Went on for a day and a night a few years back.
             Catton won on the cock-crow of Saturday.
             Mental.

SAMUEL   Don't you get hungry?
             What do you eat?

             *PERCY and ROWAN simultaneously reach into
             their trousers and brandish two cloth-wrapped
             parcels each.*

ROWAN   Pies, my friend.
             Hardly the game without pies.

             Oh, and we always lose.

PERCY   Well that's

ROWAN   Always.
             We always lose.
             Every year.

SAMUEL   Except this year, right?

PERCY   Except this year, very good!
             Nice.

ROWAN   Don't get your hopes up –

SAMUEL   Sam.

PERCY   Fat Sam!

SAMUEL   Just Sam is fine.

ROWAN   Don't get your hopes up, Fat Sam.

             Shouts from far away.

PERCY   Listen.

SAMUEL   What is it?

PERCY   We're on.

ROWAN   Here we go.

PERCY   You might want to stand back, Fat Sam.
           Don't want to get any blood on those fancy tights.

ROWAN   You hear them?

PERCY   I hear them.

           PERCY *stamps his feet. He's ready. Bellows.*

           LET'S HAVE IT THEN!

           The air catches fire.

           Time passes.

           The sky is darker, evening approaching.

           ROWAN *and* SAMUEL *stand together,* ROWAN
           *breaking off a chunk of her pie and handing it to
           him as they talk.* PERCY *stands apart, looking out,
           squinting to see, fidgeting impatiently.*

SAMUEL   I'm not saying that.
           I'm not saying you're a liar.

ROWAN   Well

SAMUEL   I'm not saying you're lying, it's just
           It's not physically possible.
           It's not in God's laws.

ROWAN   Then it's a demon.
           I never said it wasn't.

SAMUEL   Are demons born?

ROWAN   I'd say so.

SAMUEL   But from sheep though?

ROWAN   Course they are.
           You seen a sheep's hooves?

           Shows him with her hand.

           Split-foots.
           Like the devil.

SAMUEL   So what happened?

ROWAN   We heard her calling, the ewe.
I'm sleeping over at Margery's, she's Langbern's
daughter
You know the dyer?

SAMUEL   Of course.

ROWAN   Right.
So the dyer and his daughter help with the lambing
and I'm there so I help with the lambing.
They've all got blue hands, the Langberns, because
of the dye.
That's why Percy's always ragging on them
Because he's a prick.

ROWAN shouts the last word and PERCY *flips her
the bird.*

Anyway, I'm sleeping on Margery's floor, by the fire
because this is a week ago and it's colder than this.

SAMUEL   I bet.

ROWAN   Is it cold in Oxford?
Bet it's sunny in Oxford, is it?

SAMUEL   Well
Not in winter.

ROWAN   Oh no, course
Right
So I'm at Margery's and we're sleeping down by
the hearth and there's this sound, like, this terrible
sound.
And it's like

ROWAN does the noise. It's a faint cry of pain.

Like it's a long way away.
And I'm not really awake at first, but then later I am
and it's closer
And it's proper terrible now

ROWAN does the noise, louder this time.

And Margery wakes me up and she's all
'What the fuck is that?'
Like a vixen getting fucked, but foxes don't want to
fuck vixens until it warms up a bit usually, I think
Their fox knobs freeze or something, I don't know.
And Margery does this all the time and she's
shitting it.
And it's close now, outside-the-door close.

The noise.

So we go out to look, and I'm expecting to see
a full ghost
Or a huge serpent or something.
Fucking Lambton Wyrm or something.
And the yard's all blue in the moonlight and the
stars are out and there's
Something, pale, white
Staggering about the yard and bellowing out
It's a ewe, and she's in lamb
And you can tell just by the way she's moving that
something's not right
Something's gone wrong, badly wrong.
Then we catch a glance at the thing hanging out
of her
And it's huge
It's way too big, hanging too low
Just a big knot of blood and skin and shit

And then it opens

SAMUEL   Opens?

ROWAN   Like a flower
Unfurling
And in the middle of the flower there are two
heads, staring at us
Four eyes, covered in slime and
Fuck
And they look at us, and they scream.

ROWAN *tries to imitate. Terrible and bestial.*

PERCY   Shut the fuck up!

ROWAN   Sorry.
          And then the ewe just vomits, out of its arse
          Just pukes up this fucking two-headed, black-eyed,
          slimy thing.
          Gibbering and twitching.
          Margery screams, I scream.
          The ewe's been torn right open
          Heap of steaming meat on the yard.
          It was just
          So
          Much.

          SAMUEL *takes it in.*

          So it doesn't bode well for the match, is all I'm
          saying.

SAMUEL   Right.

ROWAN   Well, it doesn't sound good does it?
          Sheep gives birth to an actual monster one week
          out from the game.

PERCY   What are you talking about monster sheep?

ROWAN   Telling Samuel about the omens.
          All I'm saying is, as omens go, that's a bad one.

PERCY   Don't listen to her Sam
          She's full of that shit.

ROWAN   Mind your own beeswax, dickhead.
          I see things you don't.

PERCY   Well that's certainly true.
          She's always doing this.
          Saying weird shit.
          She's just doing it for attention.

ROWAN   Go fuck yourself.

PERCY   Ooh I would, but my hands are too cold.

          Flips ROWAN *the bird, she retaliates in kind.*

Always saying weird shit.
Seeing weird shit.
Saying weird shit about weird shit she's seen.
It's exhausting.

SAMUEL   (*To* ROWAN.) You see things?

ROWAN   What if I do?

SAMUEL   What sort of things?

ROWAN   Like that demon.
And there's been others.

PERCY   No there hasn't.

ROWAN   Er, there's been loads?

PERCY   What, there's been loads of omens?

ROWAN   Shitloads, yeah.

PERCY   Such as?

ROWAN   Birds flying backwards.

PERCY   Bollocks.

It's just windy here.

ROWAN   And when it hailed four Sundays past the stones
came down like tiny ice crosses.

PERCY   You hearing this, Fat Sam?

ROWAN   And on the church walls I've seen blood between
the stones.
Dried blood, and fresh blood.

PERCY   Totally mental.
You have gone mad like Mad John Coulyng.

SAMUEL   Did anyone else see them?

PERCY   Did they fuck!

ROWAN   Nobody else is really looking.

PERCY   See.

SAMUEL   They sound more like visions to me.

ROWAN   Same difference.

SAMUEL   I suppose so.
          There was a woman who had visions.
          Down south.

PERCY   Here we go.

SAMUEL   Sister Elizabeth Barton.

PERCY   Sister?

SAMUEL   She was a nun.

PERCY   Eh?

SAMUEL   This was a long time ago.
          When I was a boy.
          She was a servant in a rich farmhouse, and she
          started seeing things
          Things that told her about the future
          And so she became a nun.
          And she was brought to meet the King and stay
          at court.

PERCY   How absolutely fascinating, do go on?

SAMUEL   Oh, well / she

PERCY   I'm fucking joking you boring twat.

          Pause.

ROWAN   What were they? The visions?

SAMUEL   They were revelations.
          They were divine.

ROWAN   About the future?

SAMUEL   Yes.
          But not things like football games.
          Not little things.

PERCY   Mind it with the 'little'.

SAMUEL   Revelations are for catastrophes.
          And wars.
          Big things.

Like kings and queens
And treason and murder.
They're not for playing games.

ROWAN   How do you know?

PERCY   He went to Oxford, Ro
Didn't spend the last ten years in haylofts, frigging
off the chodes of farmhands.

ROWAN *is watching* SAMUEL *closely.*

Though actually
I agree.
All of that
Omen bollocks
Means fuck-all.
We've got it this year.
You can smell it in the air.
You can taste it.

Smacks his lips. ROWAN *does the same,
unconvinced, spits.*

ROWAN   You see anything?

PERCY   No.

ROWAN   You hear anything?

PERCY   Yeah, I
I think so.

ROWAN   You sure?

SAMUEL   I thought I saw something move.

PERCY   Where?

SAMUEL   In the trees.

PERCY   In those trees?

SAMUEL   I thought so.
A little while ago.
Perhaps we should –

PERCY   Perhaps we should what?

SAMUEL   Mount a small reconnaissance.

           Pause. ROWAN *and* PERCY *consider* SAMUEL.

PERCY   What is wrong with you?

           Pause. PERCY *spits.*

           I might

           Erm

           Pause.

           I might
           I might head forward, actually.

ROWAN   Yeah?

PERCY   There might have been
           If there's been a change of tactic
           If Ridley's changed tactic then we should know
           about it.
           Otherwise this could all be

ROWAN   A massive waste of time.

PERCY   Right.
           Exactly.
           What do you think?

ROWAN   Fill your boots.

PERCY   You staying here?

ROWAN   I'm staying right here.

SAMUEL   I'll come with you.

ROWAN   Why?

PERCY   You'll fucking well not.

SAMUEL   I'd like to see how the game's going.
           From up close.
           Closer, I mean.

PERCY   Well that's an absolute no.

SAMUEL   And why's that?

PERCY   You'll slow me down.
            You'll slow the whole recon-ic, the reconger

SAMUEL   The reconnaissance.

PERCY   That's right.
            You'll slow that, all of that, right down.

SAMUEL   I assure you –

ROWAN   Ah let him go.

            SAMUEL *wants to object further, but holds off.*

PERCY   I'll be straight back.
            And if Thomas wants us both forwards I'll holler.
            Like

            PERCY *makes a 'Halloo!' sound with cupped hands.*

            Like that
            Like

            'Halloo!' again.

ROWAN   I've got that.

PERCY   Yeah?

ROWAN   Absolutely.

            Pause.

PERCY   Watch him!

            ROWAN *signals she has her eye on* SAMUEL.

            I'll be back before sundown.

            ROWAN *gives two thumbs up.* PERCY *tentatively
            exits towards the Allendale goal.*

            Pause.

SAMUEL   Do you think he'll be back?

            Pause.

            Don't you think we ought to go with him?

            Long pause.

            Shall / I go –

ROWAN   How long are you up here for?

          Pause.

SAMUEL   I don't know yet.
          It's strange in London.
          Nobody really knows what's going to happen.

ROWAN   No change there then.

SAMUEL   It's different every week.
          People are nervous, nobody's really speaking.

          The King's / proclaimed

ROWAN   Yeah, I don't care about that royal shit.
          All that shit.
          Who's fucking who, whose family's on the up,
          who's on the down.
          All of it, it can all go hang as far as I care.
          We're not bothered up here, you understand?

SAMUEL   Right.
          Sorry.

ROWAN   We don't need it.
          Every time something comes up here it brings
          trouble.
          There's never anything to be gained from it.
          Just trouble.

SAMUEL   I understand.

ROWAN   I hope you do.
          If you're planning on making a home here again
          I hope you understand that.

          Pause.

          What was that you said?
          About the frost?

SAMUEL   Beg your pardon?

ROWAN   When you first turned up.
          You were talking about the / frost.

SAMUEL   Oh!
           God's breath.
           That's what they call it in the lowlands
           In the fen and mere country
           When I was on a trip away from Cambridge I stayed
           with a family in the marshland.
           Pig farmers.
           Right over the Michaelmas holidays
           Do you know the fens?

ROWAN   No.
           No, I don't know anywhere.

SAMUEL   Right.
           Well, it's flat land there, not like here.
           There you can see as far as your eyes can
           comprehend.
           You can see for miles.
           And on Christmas morning we woke up at sunrise
           and everything was white
           White on white with a white sky behind.
           But it wasn't snow, it was too cold for snow.
           It was frost.
           It was like every blade of grass and every branch of
           every tree was wearing a coat of icy spears.
           Enamelled.
           I saw a winter apple hanging from a branch like
           a horse chestnut in glass.
           I saw last year's bulrushes like an army of ghosts.
           It was as if God had blown a cold wind across the
           whole of the world and frozen it in place.
           It was beautiful.

           Anyway, that's what the farmer called it, God's
           breath.
           The breath of God.

           Pause.

ROWAN   Cambridge?

SAMUEL   That's right.

ROWAN   I thought your da sent you to Oxford?

SAMUEL   Well he did.
          But I travelled a lot, you know.
          Scholars travel a lot.

          Pause.

ROWAN   Alright then.

          You should probably be off, shouldn't you?
          Sun's almost down.

SAMUEL   I thought
          I thought I might stay on actually.

ROWAN   Stay on?

SAMUEL   Show a bit of support for the team.

ROWAN   Okay.

SAMUEL   Might even be able to help out.
          If things hot up.

ROWAN   Fine by me.
          Just

          I think he will be back.
          Just so you know.
          I think he will.
          And I think

          Pause.

          ROWAN *pulls off her scarf, and when she does,
          terrible scars are revealed across her jaw and
          neck.*

SAMUEL   What do you think?

ROWAN   I think you should be very, very careful.

          Night rushes in.

The First Night

A small fire burns on the ground before ROWAN *and*
SAMUEL. SAMUEL *crouches by it and warms his hands.*
ROWAN *has replaced her scarf.*

*They watch the fire for a time, and then turn their attention to
the sky.*

ROWAN   They're coming down tonight.

SAMUEL   They are.

ROWAN   How many have you counted?

SAMUEL   Twenty at least.
More.

ROWAN   Same.
Why so many, do you think?

SAMUEL   It's a trick of the mind.

ROWAN   It's a what?

SAMUEL   You look up at the sky, and you think you've seen
more of them than there's ever been before
You think something special's taking place but
actually –

ROWAN   Actually you've just never looked before, not
properly, and now you are.

Pause.

Bollocks.

Do they teach stars, then?

SAMUEL   A bit.
We learn the constellations and what they mean.
We learn to read them a little.

ROWAN   Reading the sky.
Fuck me.

SAMUEL   Sort of.

ROWAN   Percy can't read his own name.

          ROWAN *comes closer to* SAMUEL *and gestures*
          a swathe of the sky.

          What's that say then?

SAMUEL   What's what say?

ROWAN   (*Gestures again.*) That!

SAMUEL   What does that say?
          Erm.
          I suppose.
          It says 'It's spring in Allendale.'
          It says 'Strong-willed children are being born to
          England.'

ROWAN   It says that?

SAMUEL   In a way.
          It says
          It says something about a battle.

ROWAN   That'll be the game.

SAMUEL   I don't think so.

          There is a sound in the distance. Like an animal
          crying.

          Pause.

          I meant to ask, what happened to the thing?
          The sheep thing?

ROWAN   Don't know.
          When we went back out in the morning it was
          gone.
          Dead somewhere.
          Wolves got to it, or maybe it got the wolves.
          Wolf versus demon, who wins?

SAMUEL   That's a difficult one.

          Pause.

ROWAN   So what's that then?

           Points to a single point in the sky.

SAMUEL   Where?

ROWAN   There.
           Like a hot coal.

SAMUEL   That's

ROWAN   That's what?

SAMUEL   Nothing.

ROWAN   Nothing?

SAMUEL   I don't know.
           I really don't.

ROWAN   Some scholar.

SAMUEL   I've never / seen

PERCY   (*Shouting.*) Fuck is this!

           PERCY *enters, covered in mud and manic.*

ROWAN   Steady on.

           PERCY *stamps the fire hard, extinguishing it with
           repeated stomps.*

           What are you doing you mad bastard?

PERCY   What am I doing, what are you doing?
           Lighting a fire in the middle of the match?

ROWAN   It's cold!

PERCY   It's practically treason!
           You'll give away our position for miles!

ROWAN   Our position?
           Our position is a league away from fucking anyone,
           what does it matter who knows our position?

PERCY   (*To* SAMUEL.) This was you, wasn't it?

ROWAN   Where've you been?

PERCY   He's a traitor.
          He's a fucking spy, I knew it.

ROWAN   It was my idea actually, calm down.

PERCY   Like hell it was.

ROWAN   It was.
          I was freezing my tits off, Percy.

SAMUEL   I've got quite a sturdy cloak, so

PERCY   Shut your mouth, Catton.

ROWAN   He's no Catton.

PERCY   Sent me on a wild goose chase, didn't you Catton?

ROWAN   Fat Sam's from Allendale.

PERCY   Says you.

ROWAN   It was your idea to go wandering off, anyway!
          Where've you been?

PERCY   Oh everywhere, mate.
          Every-fucking-where.
          I've been to Peth Hill, I've been to the Stouts
          I've been round Thornley Woods, where this
          bastard said he'd seen them
          I've been round Thornley Woods three times and
          there's dick-all there.
          Nothing.
          Nobody.
          I've scrambled up the dyke and I've slipped down it
          Slipped down it then slipped back up again.
          I feel like my heart's going to explode from my
          chest.
          Walking round in circles for hours in the dark
          Listening for the church bell, so I could work out
          which direction I was facing in and you know what?

          (*To* SAMUEL.) You know what?

ROWAN   What?

PERCY   I couldn't hear a thing.

ROWAN   So?

PERCY   So why's that then?

ROWAN   You're a deaf bastard

PERCY   Or
           Witchcraft.

ROWAN   Or, an ear full of river-mud.

PERCY   One of his Catton witches muffled the bell.
           Knobbling the opposition's best players.
           That's textbook Catton that is.

SAMUEL   That's not true.

ROWAN   Of course it's not.

PERCY   Whose side are you on?

ROWAN   On the side of you getting lost not necessarily
           being evidence of Satan's intercession on behalf of
           Catton's football prospects.

PERCY   Oh yeah?

           Squares up to SAMUEL.

           It's not a joke.
           Cos I saw something, when I was out there, in
           the dark.
           I thought it was the others at first but they were so
           far off, and then I realised they were carrying lights.
           Carrying torches and I thought, that's not right.
           Why would our lads be carrying torches?
           Why would our lads be carrying torches on
           match day?
           They wouldn't, would they?
           Would they?

SAMUEL   I don't know.

PERCY   So I stood and I watched them.
           All up the valley side by Thornley.

           A train of lights, bobbing along the tops road.
           Must have been two-score of them.

So how do you explain that, Catton?
How you going to explain that?

PERCY grabs SAMUEL by the scruff of his neck.

ROWAN   Fuck's sake!

PERCY   I'm on to you.
I know what you're up to.

ROWAN   Leave him be!

PERCY drops SAMUEL and he falls back, coughing.

PERCY   They can do that sort of thing, witches.
Take away your hearing and turn you around.
Turn you about in the dark.
Next thing you know you're trussed up, bollock-naked at a Witches' Sabbath and we've lost the fucking football!

ROWAN   Stop that.

SAMUEL   I wouldn't know.

PERCY   No?
Don't you have witches in Oxford.

ROWAN   Percy.

SAMUEL   Well I'm yet to meet one, put it like that.

PERCY   Home to get your fix?

ROWAN   That's enough.
Enough.
I don't want to hear it.
I don't want to hear about any of it.

Pause.

PERCY   Sorry, Ro.

ROWAN   Ah, you're alright.

ROWAN kicks the remnants of the fire.

PERCY spits.

PERCY   You got water?

ROWAN *hands him her pouch.* PERCY *drinks from it, and then empties it onto his face.*

Cold!
Fuck that's cold!

ROWAN   Steady.

PERCY *washes the mud from his face.*

Did you see anything?

PERCY

No.

Pause.

ROWAN   It must be nearly over.

PERCY   Yeah, maybe.

ROWAN   Day and a night.

PERCY   Like '41.

ROWAN   Well
Wake me when it's over.

ROWAN *begins to bed down by the remnants of the fire.*

PERCY   You what?

ROWAN   I'm having a kip.

PERCY   What if you're needed?

ROWAN   Then you'll wake me up, won't you?

PERCY   What about you Catton?
Off home to your swan-feather mattress?

SAMUEL   That's not a thing.

And I'm staying.

PERCY   Suit yourself.

ROWAN   Christ it's cold.

PERCY   Could be worse.

ROWAN   That's not as much of a consolation as you think it is.

             ROWAN *lies on her back, staring at the sky.*

             Pause.

             That a sickle, would you say?

PERCY   That a what?

ROWAN   The moon.
             Is that a sickle moon would you say?

PERCY   Looks like.

SAMUEL   I'd say it's a day shy.

ROWAN   Fat Sam reads the sky.

PERCY   That a fact?

SAMUEL   It's not reading.
             It's just looking, really.

ROWAN   What's one day shy of a sickle?

SAMUEL   I don't think there's a word for that.

PERCY   Opposite of a harvest moon.
             What's the opposite of a harvest?

SAMUEL
             I don't think there's a word for that either.

             Time passes. The dark deepens.

             ROWAN *and* SAMUEL *are asleep, a few paces
             apart.* PERCY *stands looking out.*

             PERCY *claps his hands together to keep warm.
             Stamps his feet. He retrieves a crust of pie from his
             pocket and finishes it greedily.*

             He sings under his breath.

PERCY   Pastime with good company
             I love and shall until I die;

Complain who will, but none deny
If God be pleased then so shall I.

(*Louder.*) If God be pleased then so shall I.

A BOY *enters, carrying a flaming torch in one
hand and a length of birch in the other.*

BOY   Hello.

              PERCY *turns, shaken.*

              I said, hello.

PERCY   Hello.

BOY   Are you watching the game?

PERCY   Am I?
              Oh, er, no, I'm
              I'm playing.

BOY   Oh.
              Right.
              What were you singing?

PERCY   Just a song
              Football song.

BOY   I see.

PERCY   I'm Percy Lamrose.

BOY   I know who you are.

PERCY   Do you?

BOY   You're at the cottage by Woolly Burn.

PERCY   That's right.
              And who are you?

BOY   I'm Robert.
              I'd shake your hand, but

              Indicates hands are full.

              You're on my father's list.
              He wants to speak to you.

PERCY   Oh that's, that's
         And who / are you?

BOY   We're beating the bounds.
         I'm here with my father and my uncle.
         This is my birch.
         Do you like it?

PERCY   Yes.
         It's nice and
         Straight.

BOY   I want to chase partridge with it but my father
         won't let me.

PERCY   That's a shame.

BOY   We've been halfway round the Catton bounds
         tonight already.

PERCY   Oh, I saw you!
         I saw you in procession.

BOY   Did you?

PERCY   I did, I was lost and then
         So that was you!

BOY   Must have been!

PERCY   But it's not
         It's not Rogation, it's Whitsun.

BOY   I beg your pardon?

PERCY   It's Whitsuntide, it's not the Gang-Days.
         Why are you beating the bounds?
         You beat the bounds two months back.

BOY   Well those were the old bounds, these are the new.
         King's orders.

PERCY   How can you change them?
         The bounds are the bounds, they
         They stay the same, they don't change.
         What's the point of having them if they don't stay
         the same?

BOY   Are you questioning the King's orders?

PERCY   No, of course I'm not
           I'm sorry
           I just don't understand why you're
           What's your name?

BOY   Robert.

PERCY   Robert what?

BOY   I'm not telling.

PERCY   Where's your father?
           Why does he want to speak to me?

BOY   He wants to speak to all husbandmen affected by
           the boundary change.

PERCY   What change?
           What are you changing?

BOY   The bounds between Allendale and Catton.
           We're moving them south a little way.

PERCY   How far south?

BOY   To just beyond the Shield Burn.

PERCY   But that's
           Then I won't even be in Allendale any more
           I'll be in
           I won't

           Well, you can't do that.
           You can't do it.

BOY   I'm sorry you're upset.

PERCY   Upset?
           That's my home
           It was my father's home
           I was born there, do you see?
           I was born there.
           You can't change it.
           You can't change it just like that.

Show me.
Show me, I want to see it.

BOY   There's nothing to show.
           It's done.

PERCY   Show me a chart or a map.
           Show me it on ink and parchment!

BOY   It's not written down.
           It's just in here –

           BOY *gestures to his temple.*

           Father says a boy's mind is better than any
           parchment.
           It'll last for years and years up here and nobody
           can lose it or burn it.
           It'll last as long as I remember the line I beat with
           this birch.
           It's clever, isn't it?

PERCY   Is it?

           Pause.

           There is a terrible, bestial sound.

BOY   Oh! That's my father calling.

PERCY   What?

BOY   I need to go.

PERCY   No, wait, you have to tell him.

           The BOY *runs off.*

           Tell him I'm not having it!
           Tell him!
           Tell him it's not moving!
           Tell him I am Percy Lamrose, son of Allendale

           And I'll cut his fucking throat!

           *A bell tolls in the distance. Louder and louder and
           louder.*

The Second Day

Bright white sunlight bakes the earth. PERCY *lies spread-eagle on the ground.* ROWAN *enters and stands over him, shakes her head.*

She takes a pouch of water and empties it over his face.

PERCY   What? Fuck!
               Ro!

ROWAN   Sleeping on the job.

PERCY   What time is it?

ROWAN   Past ten.

PERCY   Is it over?

ROWAN   Nope.

PERCY   No?
               Have they come past?

ROWAN   Nope.

PERCY   Then how do you know it's not over?

ROWAN   There was a man.
               Down by the burn, I went to top up.

               Indicates water, swigs.

               Never seen him before, said his name was John.
               'John,' I said
               'That's right.'
               'Well, that doesn't narrow it down that much, mate.
               Out of the eighty-odd men in this valley fifty-four
               are called John, so…'
               Not from the valley.
               Spectator.
               Except he's not spectating because he's packed in
               and he's off home.
               Said he's not the stomach for it.

PERCY   Hot.
               Jesus.

ROWAN   Yeah, there's that as well.

PERCY   What did he tell you?

ROWAN   Said he'd seen some not-nice things and he was
heading home.
Said he'd had enough and it was a crime to keep
playing after that and what was wrong with us.

PERCY   What had he seen?

ROWAN   I didn't ask.

PERCY   You got anything to eat?

ROWAN   Few crumbs.
Must be over soon.

PERCY   Yeah, maybe.

ROWAN   It's what Ridders said, isn't it?
'Wear them down, and finish them off'
They're not like our lads, they're not used to a long
game.
We'll run them ragged, and when the time is right
Bang!
Smash the post on Catton Green and back to
The Cock in time for a sing-song and an absolute
fuckload of braised beef.

PERCY   Maybe.

ROWAN   Sound alright?

PERCY   Maybe.

ROWAN   What?

PERCY   What nothing.

ROWAN   Why you looking like that?

PERCY   Like what?

ROWAN   Like someone's come round and shagged your cat?

PERCY *looks around him. Remembers with a start.*

PERCY   There was a boy.
           Last night, there was a boy.

ROWAN   What, here?

PERCY   Yes here.
           You were asleep but he was here.

ROWAN   Out on his own?

PERCY   No, he was with his dad.
           They were beating the bounds.

ROWAN   You what?

PERCY   But it wasn't his dad.
           It was horrible.

ROWAN   And he was beating the bounds?

PERCY   He had his birch with him.
           Said they were moving the boundary line.

ROWAN   Right, well that's mental.

PERCY   Did you see anyone?
           Like a procession?

ROWAN   No.
           It's Whitsun.

PERCY   That's what I told him.

ROWAN   It's weeks since the Gang-Days.

PERCY   That's what I told him.

ROWAN   Why would they do it again?

PERCY   He said something about the King.

ROWAN   Could you have been dreaming, Perce?

PERCY   No! I don't sleep on the job.
           Well, I wasn't
           Look, I wasn't dreaming, alright?

ROWAN   Did he say who he was?

PERCY   Said his name was Robert.

              PERCY *springs to his feet.*

              Where's he gone?

ROWAN   Fat Sam?
              I don't know.

PERCY   He's left us.

ROWAN   What if he has?
              Thought you'd be glad.

PERCY   Yeah but why now?
              Christ it's hot.
              Water?

              ROWAN *hands him the pouch and he drinks from it.*

              He said it was something about the King.
              Something from London.

ROWAN   Who did?

PERCY   The boy.

ROWAN   Your boy Robert.

PERCY   Yes.
              What, and you don't think it's strange?
              Can't get rid of Catton until we're both asleep and
              he scarpers?
              Something's afoot.

ROWAN   Afoot, is it?

PERCY   Very much so.
              Very much fucking afoot.

              PERCY *drains the last of the pouch.*

ROWAN   You want to go easy on that.
              The burn's practically dry.

PERCY   You what?

ROWAN   Trickle when I got down there.

PERCY   Two days ago it was two-foot deep and frozen
          near solid.

ROWAN   By all means take a look for yourself.

PERCY   No I'm not leaving my position, Ro.
          What's this all about?

ROWAN   This what?

PERCY   All this –

          Weather.

ROWAN   Search me.

PERCY   I don't like it.
          We're shite when it's hard, you said so yourself.

          Someone's playing around with us.
          Someone's pulling on our pricks, you hear me?
          Hoar frost at Whitsun and then this.
          Skin's all
          I can feel it.
          I mean, what's the chances of this?
          Without someone
          You know what I'm talking about.

ROWAN   I know what you're talking about.
          And I want you to stop right now.

PERCY   Yeah
          Yeah right.

          SAMUEL *enters*.

ROWAN   Alright.

PERCY   Where've you been?

SAMUEL   Good morning to you.

PERCY   Don't get smart with me!
          Where've you been?
          I said, where have you been, Catton?

          SAMUEL *throws down a knapsack*.

SAMUEL   Bringing you your breakfast.

           PERCY *cautiously checks the bag, finds a loaf of
           bread and begins to eat.*

           Provisions for the players.

ROWAN   Thank Christ.

           ROWAN *tucks in too.*

           Where'd you
           Where'd you get this?

SAMUEL   Robinson's.

PERCY   You've been to town?

SAMUEL   Yes, well, only as far as Robinson's.
           Rest of town looks boarded up.
           Like they're expecting trouble.

ROWAN   Always like that when the game's on.

SAMUEL   Anyway.
           New batch this morning.
           You're welcome.

PERCY   Did you see anyone?

SAMUEL   Only the woman at Blackett's mill.

ROWAN   His daughter.

PERCY   What did she say?

SAMUEL   She said
           She said there'd been trouble at Hallstile Cross.
           Said someone was killed.
           Tom Perdew.

ROWAN   Jesus, Tom Perdew!

SAMUEL   Crushed, apparently.
           Something about a bad tackle.
           His body's in the chapel now.

PERCY   Those bastards.

           He can't have been twenty.

ROWAN   No.

PERCY   Anything else?
          Where are they now?

SAMUEL   She didn't say.

PERCY   Hallstile Cross's north of here though.
          It's well north.
          That means it's closer, it's Catton-side.
          Get in!
          Any water?

SAMUEL   No, sorry.
          It's hot.

ROWAN   We'd noticed.

SAMUEL   It's strange weather here these days.
          Hotter than Oxford, I'd expect.

PERCY   All the better to sear the skins of those Catton
          bastards.

          It's coming home for the team of '53!
          The sons of Allendale are coming through!

SAMUEL   Oh, I saw that procession by the way.

          Pause.

PERCY   You what?

SAMUEL   Last night, when you were in the woods, you
          mentioned a procession of torches.
          I saw them, in the churchyard.
          Clergy for the most part, and some royal officials.
          They're marking the new boundaries, I think.

PERCY   What new boundaries?

SAMUEL   I don't know.
          I expect it's something to do with the Act.

PERCY   What are you talking about?

SAMUEL   Parliament's new Act.
          The King's Act.

ROWAN   Oh here we go.
           Not interested.

PERCY   What you mean the King's Act?

SAMUEL   Edward.

PERCY   I know who the fucking King is, Catton.
           Don't get smart with me.
           What is this?

ROWAN   Doesn't concern us.

PERCY   Like hell it doesn't.
           Talk, Catton.

SAMUEL   I don't know much about it.
           It's just an Act of Parliament.
           Consolidating the King's lands.

PERCY   That child?

SAMUEL   Well, it's Cranmer really.
           He knows the King's not got long.

PERCY   Who's Cranmer?

SAMUEL   You don't know who Thomas Cranmer is?

ROWAN   Don't give a weasel's last shit about / any of that.

PERCY   Shut up, Ro!

SAMUEL   But he's the Archbishop of Canterbury.
           He's the most powerful man in England.

PERCY   And what's an archbishop got to do with my
           father's house?

SAMUEL   Your what?

ROWAN   Perce?

SAMUEL   It's part of the transfer of authority.

PERCY   Transfer of what?

SAMUEL   Priest to parson
           Parson to squire

          Sack the churches, sell what you can
          Burn what you can't.
          Mutatis mutandis.

PERCY   What does that mean, Catton?

SAMUEL   It means the changes are being made.
          It means there's nothing you can do about it.

PERCY   How can you say that?

SAMUEL   It's the truth.

PERCY   Wipe that fucking grin off your face.

SAMUEL   I'm not smiling, believe me.
          But that's life just at the moment.

PERCY   That's life?

ROWAN   Steady.

PERCY   How can he be so fucking casual about it?

ROWAN   Just eat your bread.

PERCY   Fuck the bread!
          I wouldn't touch it, if he's had his bastard hands
          on it!

          PERCY *throws the loaf to the ground and hoofs it
          across the soil.*

          They're taking my name!
          They're taking it all, that's what he said.

SAMUEL   (*Incredulous, half-laughing.*) I didn't say anything
          like that.

PERCY   I said wipe that fucking smile off your face!

          PERCY *launches himself at* SAMUEL. SAMUEL
          moves aside, and when PERCY *lunges again*
          SAMUEL *delivers a fast, precise knee to his
          bollocks.* PERCY *crumples to the ground.*

          God's fucking
          Blood.

Ow.
I'll put you in the ground, Catton.

ROWAN   Leave it!
He's done nothing to you.
He doesn't know what you're on about.

PERCY   Doesn't he?

ROWAN   No! And neither do I!

PERCY *drags himself back to his feet.*

PERCY   Tell him to shut his mouth then.
This is my life.
This is where I'm from, and he's saying it's
changing just like that.
That the Boy-King can take it just like that?

SAMUEL   Well he can.
It's not even taking because it's all his anyway.
He'll teach you that, if you didn't know it already.

ROWAN   Enough, Fat Sam!
Leave it now.

SAMUEL   They say his father broke from Rome but his son
broke more than that.
He broke the whole chain.

ROWAN *tries to hold* PERCY *back.*

I'm sorry.

PERCY   What are you sorry for?
Catton? Eh?
What have you got to be sorry for?

SAMUEL   I'm sorry you're seeing it for the first time.
I didn't come here to upset you.

PERCY   What was that?

SAMUEL   I'm sorry if I've upset you, / I didn't

PERCY   You said you didn't come to upset me
             So what did you come for?
             When did you say you got here?

ROWAN   He didn't say anything.

SAMUEL   Last week.

PERCY   Last week, when last week?

ROWAN   What's it matter?
             Drop it, Perce, you're going off on one.

PERCY   Up from London, that's what he said.
             He said they're up from London.

SAMUEL   No I didn't.

PERCY   Royal whatever
             Business.

             He said that!
             From the south.

SAMUEL   I didn't say that.

ROWAN   He didn't say that.
             I didn't hear him say that and neither did you.

PERCY   Not him, I'm talking about the fucking boy!

SAMUEL   I don't know what you're talking about.

             PERCY *raises his hand to point at* SAMUEL,
             accusing.

PERCY   He's with them.
             He's come with the procession.
             They said they wanted to speak to me, and he's
             their little watcher.

             As PERCY *steps towards* SAMUEL *he has
             a twinge of pain in his groin and winces. Then
             freezes. And smiles.*

             Oh! Oh-ho!
             Now I'm thinking.

Now I'm remembering.
And it's not good news for you Fat Sam.
You do not want me remembering.
Rowan, you can help me with this?

ROWAN   With what?

PERCY   Nicholas Jaane.
What do you remember about Nicholas Jaane?

ROWAN   Not much.

PERCY   Really?
Because I remember a song.
Little song.
You know the song, Fat Sam?

SAMUEL   No.

PERCY   You remember a song, Ro?

ROWAN   No.

PERCY   I thought you were good with songs?
Always singing, our Rowan.
Well I don't remember it all either
But it started 'Nicholas Jaane, Nicholas Jaane'
And at the end of it he didn't have a dick any more.
Some kind of
Christmas accident.

ROWAN   You what?
What the fuck are you talking about?
A Christmas / accident

PERCY   Yes a fucking Christmas accident what's so funny
about that?

ROWAN   It's ridiculous.

PERCY   Coal from a fire or something
Hot chestnut,
Burnt his dick so bad he never so much as went
near a girl.
That's why he lives out there on his own in that big
old house.

SAMUEL   That's not true.

ROWAN   Some schoolboys made up a song about Nick Jaane
having a 'Christmas accident' whatever the hell that
is and because of that Sam's
What?
Catton?
You're touched, Percy Lamrose.
The heat's fogged your brain.

PERCY   And you
You know that don't you?
You know he's not Nick Jaane's son   .
You knew the moment he arrived.
This heat's not fogged my brain
It's scalded it clear.

ROWAN   Has it really.
You should get going, Samuel.

SAMUEL   No.

ROWAN   I think it's time for you to leave now.
You're not playing the game, you shouldn't even
be here.
Get yourself home.
Percy's not himself.

SAMUEL   I'm staying here.

ROWAN   You're going.

           ROWAN *looks into* SAMUEL's *eyes for a long
           moment.*

           You're going now.
           Alright?
           Go now or I'll never forgive you.
           Now Samuel!

           ROWAN *pushes* SAMUEL. *He resists, but feebly.*

           Fuck off, Sam!
           Get the fuck out of here, alright, Oxford boy.

SAMUEL   I'm staying.

> ROWAN *grabs* SAMUEL*'s head and pushes hers against it.*

ROWAN   Listen, listen.
Something's going to happen now that's not for you.
No, listen.
It isn't meant for you, but if you're not careful it'll suck you in.
I've seen it.

PERCY   C'mon Catton!

ROWAN   Run, Fat Sam.
Please.

PERCY   What are you playing at.

ROWAN   Last chance, Sam.

SAMUEL   I'm staying.
I don't need help from a

ROWAN   From a what?
Finish what you were going to say.

SAMUEL   I know it's not your fault, but
But you can't help me.

> ROWAN *stares at* SAMUEL. *Then decides.*
> ROWAN *rounds on* PERCY.

ROWAN   I've never seen him before.
I've never seen him.
Nicholas Jaane's a eunuch.
I'd never seen him before he walked onto this field yesterday.
Maybe he is Catton or maybe he's come to beat the bounds
I don't care because he's leaving.
He's leaving right now if I have to drag him away with me because there's something in you this morning that I've seen before.

PERCY   I knew it.
         You lied to me, Ro.

ROWAN   What if I did?

PERCY   You know who he is, don't you?

ROWAN   Not a clue.
         Never seen him before.

PERCY   Who is he?

ROWAN   Read my lips, Percy.
         I've never seen him before in my life.

PERCY   Liar.

ROWAN   I've / never seen / him before in my fucking / life!

PERCY   Liar
         Liar
         Liar

ROWAN   You're a prick.

         PERCY *walks to* ROWAN *and rips her scarf from her neck.*

PERCY   And you're a scold.

         ROWAN *instinctively goes to cover her scars.*

ROWAN   Fuck you.
         Fuck you, Percy Lamrose.

PERCY   Maybe you should think about that next time.
         Think about your tongue before you lash me with
         it, eh?
         Or next time I might not be there to help you.

ROWAN   What help were you to me?
         When they dragged me out of my father's house on
         Plough Monday?
         When they tore the clothes off my back and took
         shears to my hair?
         How about when they fitted the bridle?
         You ever seen a bridle, Sam?

SAMUEL   Once.

ROWAN   Then you know.

PERCY   Ro, I –

ROWAN   Where were you, Perce?
          When they lowered the cage around my head
          Crushed the bit against my tongue
          Sealed it with a hot iron until my skin blistered.
          What help were you to me then?
          When Edith, and Joan and Marion stood under the
          shelter of the sycamore while it rained so hard it was
          like a witch-pricking and when I dragged my shame
          along the river path gagging on an iron plate?
          What help were you then?
          What help were any of you?

SAMUEL   I'm sorry
          That was wrong. I'm sure –
          If I'd been / here.

ROWAN   No offence, Samuel whatever your name is but
          I doubt you'd have raised a finger.
          No offence but I've seen your kind before.

SAMUEL   What was your [crime]
          What were you accused of?

ROWAN   Told one too many suitors to piss off.
          Isn't that right?

PERCY   It was nothing to do with me!
          I told you that!

ROWAN   No?
          No, well
          Maybe it doesn't have to be.
          Maybe you just have to
          Stand by and do fuck-all.

PERCY   I wanted to / tell them

ROWAN   Oh hold your peace.
          You're a small man, that's what that day taught me.

It's a town of small men, it's a country of small men,
but even then, even then you're one of the smallest.

Backward rear fucking defence.
Answer me this, Catton, how shit does he have to
be at football to get stuck all the way out here with
the village scold?
The village [whore]?

I'm done.
I'm done with this.
They can play till the end of the world, for all I care.
Let them.
I hope they all drown like John Hipper.

(*Laughing*.) He was a prick as well.

PERCY *is deflated, defeated*.

Look after yourself, Fat Sam.
Hope you get out of here alive.
I wish I had.

PERCY   Where you going?

ROWAN   Down to The Cock.
Gonna get wrecked.

PERCY   I'll see you there after?
When we've won.

ROWAN

Alright then.
See you, Perce.

PERCY   See you, Ro.

ROWAN *goes to leave*.

ROWAN   Oh, quick question
One for you, Fat Sam
And it's the last thing you'll hear from me.

What happened to her?

SAMUEL   Who?

ROWAN   Elizabeth.
         The nun, with the revelations, what happened to her?

SAMUEL

         They killed her.
         They hung her at Tyburn.

         Pause.

ROWAN   Right.
         Alright then.

         ROWAN *exits, raising one hand in a 'goodbye' as
         she goes.*

         SAMUEL *watches* PERCY. *He goes over to put
         a hand on his shoulder;* PERCY *flinches away,
         then allows it.*

         The sky is darker than it was before.

PERCY   We've lost the light.

         PERCY *squints ahead of him, tears in his eyes.*

SAMUEL   Are you [alright]?

PERCY   Don't
         Say a word.

         Pause.

SAMUEL   There's a golden chain that runs through all things.
         Did you know that?

PERCY   You fucking?

SAMUEL   Did they ever teach you that?
         A great chain of being.
         Bright gold rings, a ladder from the earth to the sky.
         You can't see it but it's there, it's all around you
         Holding you in place.
         Can you feel it?

PERCY

SAMUEL   I can feel it.
         It runs through every single thing in creation.

From the mud under your feet to the stars over
your head.
From peasant to king.
From king to God Almighty.

You want to know why you're here and they're there.
Why you're so far outside the circle.
That's why.
It holds you in place.

PERCY   I've felt it.

SAMUEL   That's good.

PERCY   I felt it once, but now –

SAMUEL   Now it's breaking.

Can you feel it breaking?

PERCY   Maybe.
Yes.

The sky darkens.

What is this?
It's a trick.

SAMUEL   Percy, listen to me.
I need to tell you something.

PERCY   Yes.

SAMUEL   I'm not from Catton.

PERCY   No?

SAMUEL   And I'm not part of the procession.

PERCY   Who are you then?

SAMUEL   I'm a Catholic.

Do you understand me?
Do you understand what that means?

PERCY   A Catholic?

SAMUEL   And Nicholas Jaane isn't a eunuch.
He's a priest.

I want you to know, Percy.
I want you to know that you can trust me.

PERCY   I don't know you.

SAMUEL   I know you don't, but I need you.
We need you.
We need someone in the village we can trust.
We need someone who has a house outside of
the village.
Someone who won't be suspected,
We need someone who's anonymous.
That's why I'm here.

PERCY   Anonymous?

SAMUEL   Things in London are terrible.
They're sacking the houses of high-born families.
Powerful families.
They're taking them.
Torturing them.
They're putting men to fire.

PERCY   Catholic men.

SAMUEL   And what of that?
What have the good reformers of this village ever
given you?

PERCY   Nothing but

SAMUEL   Nothing but

PERCY   But

SAMUEL   But what?
I need you to help me make a chain.

PERCY   A chain?

SAMUEL   Not a gold chain, but a chain of men
Good men
Safe houses
From London to Mary's lands in the north.
There are only a few of us now but there are
more coming.
A lot more.

PERCY   Of you?

SAMUEL   That's right.

PERCY   You were at Oxford?

SAMUEL   I was in Spain.

PERCY   You're a traitor.

SAMUEL   They told you that.

PERCY   You're a popish traitor.

SAMUEL   That's what they told you but it's not true.

PERCY   No?

SAMUEL   It's not true.
I'm not a traitor.
I'm just trying to save men's lives.

PERCY   This is your fault.

SAMUEL   What is?

PERCY   This!
All of this!
They're taking my name, do you hear me?
They're taking my home?

SAMUEL   And who do you think is doing that?

PERCY   I don't know.

SAMUEL   The King.

PERCY   Yes.

SAMUEL   The King is.
And he's taking mine.
He's taking everything.
My father fled to France but my uncle
My uncle is dead and the King is responsible.

PERCY   It's you lot are responsible.
You're a liar.
You've admitted it.
You lied to me before and you're lying now.

SAMUEL   I'm not lying to you, Percy.

PERCY   I see you.
           I see all of you.
           When I was a boy I'd walk through the doors of the
           church and I thought I was dead already
           I thought I'd passed in my sleep and woken up in
           another world
           Like you'd torn the shitty cloth from the wall of my
           life and behind it was just all majesty and sweet,
           sweet smells
           And even then, even then I thought
           How does one house have all of this?
           How does even God's house have all of this?
           Even then I knew, I reckon.
           I reckon I knew you were all full of shit.
           Men like you.
           When I was a boy I saw men like you.
           Papist men.
           Roman men.
           They made small of me and they made small of
           this town.
           They made small of my father.
           Men like you, boys like you.
           You got rich and fat, Fat Sam, through men like me.
           Well I've had enough.
           I hope they find you, and I hope they find Nicholas
           fucking Jaane, and I hope you squeal when they
           roast you.
           I hope you scream.

SAMUEL   I'm not your enemy, Percy Lamrose.

PERCY   Well you look a lot fucking like him!
           And you talk like him.
           And you dress like him.
           And you
           You

SAMUEL   I've seen it before.
           What they're doing to you.
           Once you were Allendale, now you're Catton.

Once you were a Lamrose of Woolly Burn
And what are you now?
I've seen men like you, all used up.

PERCY   That's not true.

SAMUEL   No?

PERCY   Of course not.
I just want what's mine.

SAMUEL   I need you, Percy.
I need you now.

PERCY   I don't understand.

Pause.

SAMUEL   Is that how you feel when you see her?
Like someone's torn the cloth from your life?
Is it?
Or like you're burning?

PERCY   Her? Who's her?
Ro?
You don't know anything about her.

SAMUEL   I know you feel guilt for what happened

PERCY   That wasn't my fault

SAMUEL   Of course not, / but

PERCY   That was nothing to do with me!
I only said, and then
Then it was
That was my

SAMUEL   That was your what?
Your friends? Your father?

PERCY   Shut up!
Shut your mouth.

SAMUEL   And there was absolutely nothing you could
have done?

PERCY   No.

SAMUEL   Nothing on this earth?

PERCY   Maybe, I don't –

SAMUEL   You could have stopped them with a word.
But you didn't.
You chose not to.
You chose this.

PERCY   I didn't choose anything!

I don't choose, I don't –
(*Sobs*.)
I never –

SAMUEL   There'll be worse to come
For her, and for you.

PERCY   Not one more word.
I swear it.

SAMUEL   You think you've lost it all
But there's so much more to lose

PERCY   Shut it! Shut it!

PERCY clamps his hands to his ears.

SAMUEL   They'll
Take
Everything

PERCY   Argh!

*With a cry, PERCY lunges at SAMUEL. They fight
for a moment, SAMUEL offering little resistance
as PERCY wrestles him to the ground. He begins
to punch him.*

Is this what you want?
This what you after?
Is it?
Is it?

Eventually PERCY*'s hands are around* SAMUEL*'s neck.*

You can't have any more.
Any of you!
There's nothing left to take.
Just dirt
Just mud
And so much
Nothing!

The sky darkens.

PERCY *takes* SAMUEL*'s head in his hands and slams it over and over again on the earth. He does it until* SAMUEL*'s neck is clearly broken. He does it until* SAMUEL *is dead.*

PERCY *crouches over the body, shaking.*

The sky darkens. Night arrives.

Oh God
Oh God

PERCY *is panicking. He goes to the body and tries to lift it. To drag it. As he struggles he trips over something embedded in the mud.*

He drops the body to look.

Pause.

It's a large iron ring, caked in mud.

He pulls the ring and a trapdoor opens in the earth.

He stares into the blackness. He looks around him.

He drags the body to the lip of the pit and then tips it in.

He closes the trapdoor.

It's now very dark indeed.

Time passes.

The Second Night

PERCY *is slumped over the closed earth. He murmurs the song, half-delirious.*

PERCY   Pastime with good company
             I love
             I love and shall until I die
             Until I die.

             Noises from the dark.

             Ro?
             Ro?

             Who's there?

             The BOY *enters.*

BOY   Hello again.

PERCY   What?

BOY   I said, hello again.

PERCY   Hello.

BOY   I saw you earlier, didn't I.

PERCY   Last night.

BOY   That's right.

PERCY   You were
             You were

BOY   We were beating the bounds, but we're finished now.
             I've got the whole valley

             Taps head.

             Right here.

             He extends his hand to PERCY.

             Robert Gray.

             PERCY *takes it.*

PERCY   Percy
          Percy Lamrose.

BOY   That's right, I remember.

          Your hands are very dirty, aren't they?

PERCY   They're
          I'm a player.
          In the game.

BOY   Are you?
          You're a long way away from it.

PERCY   I am.

BOY   I've been watching them.
          Just outside the village.
          I was watching them with my father.

PERCY   Did you
          Did you see who was winning?

BOY   Oh no.
          It was just a lot of shouting men.
          Just a lot of men shouting and hitting each other.

PERCY   But where were they?

BOY   It looked horrid.

PERCY   It can be.

BOY   Are you feeling alright?

PERCY   I'm feeling fine.

BOY   It's just you're

PERCY   I'm what.

BOY   You just

PERCY   What?

BOY   Anyway, we're putting a stop to it.

PERCY   You're putting a stop to it?
          You're putting a stop to what?

BOY   There's a procla
           A procela

PERCY   A proclamation, what proclamation?

BOY   An order.
           There's a new order.

PERCY   Whose order?

BOY   All games on Whitsun- and Rogation-tide to be
           outlawed.

PERCY   No.
           No that can't be.
           Who's
           Who has ordered it?

BOY   The King.

           So this will be the last one, I expect.

           My father's already delivered the procl,
           procerlamation.

PERCY   Has he?

           PERCY *is trembling.*

BOY   I'd best be going.

PERCY   No you don't.
           I want to see your father.
           Where is he?

BOY   I need to get back.

           PERCY *lunges at the* BOY *and grabs him by his
           collar.*

PERCY   Where is he?
           I want to
           I need to speak to him.
           I need to speak to him right now.

BOY   He's
           He's

PERCY   Where is he?
Bring him to me.
Fetch him now.
Now!
Or I'll whip the skin off your back.
Go!

PERCY throws the BOY *down and he scrambles to his feet and exits.*

The chain has broken.

PERCY is alone. He stares out and up at the sky.

He's watching something impossible. It bathes him in a deep red light.

After a time, SAMUEL *joins him. He looks pretty well, considering.* PERCY *closes his eyes and steadies himself.*

What is it?

SAMUEL   I don't know.

PERCY   I thought you read the sky.

SAMUEL   I do.

PERCY   So what do you see?

SAMUEL   What do I see?
What do you see?

PERCY   How are you here?

SAMUEL puts his finger to his lips.

SAMUEL   Shhhh.
What do you see?

PERCY   I see
Blood.
I see
Blood and gold.
I see a crown.

SAMUEL   Good.

PERCY   I see a crown of blood and fire.
          I see
          I see a, a
          I see

SAMUEL   Tell me.

PERCY   I see two willow trees leaning into a dell
          I see a ditch at the edge of a field on the skirt of
          a wood and I see four legs in the moonlight tossed
          into it.
          I see two children, half-in and half-out of a blanket
          of leaves and I see the marks on their necks like
          bramble juice.

SAMUEL   Good, and?

PERCY   I see a man in a pit on the morning of his death
          Hunted by the law.
          His mind's a millstone worn flat and smooth.
          He's heavy and he's tired and they've closed in so
          tight around him.
          He's afraid that if he stands up, that's it.
          He's scared he's going to die.
          He is going to die.
          He dies.

SAMUEL   And?

PERCY   Bodies sink into the peat
          Wives and daughters and fathers and sons
          Secret and destroyed

          Pushed under the black water with broken shanks.

SAMUEL   And?

PERCY   A boat smashes off the holy rocks by Lindisfarne.
          Then another.
          Another.
          Another.

SAMUEL   And?

PERCY   A fire starts at Carr Shield fell and takes and takes
          until the horizon line is in flames.
          And it's burning so bright until it's the middle of
          a flame and the whole world is the wick.
          Until there's nothing else except sheets and sheets
          of fire and smoke.

SAMUEL   And what else?

PERCY   What else?

SAMUEL   What else do you see?

PERCY   I don't see anything else.

SAMUEL   Liar.

PERCY   I see
          Holes, in everything
          I just keep finding holes.
          Below me and above me.

SAMUEL   I know.

          PERCY *is weeping, he wipes his eyes to clear
          them.*

PERCY   What do you see?

SAMUEL   I see that.
          I see that light right there in the sky.

          He points up.

          It means a war coming.
          There's a war coming and people are going to die.
          People like you are going to die in their thousands.
          That's what it means.

PERCY   Is that what you see?

SAMUEL   I think so.

          I see a toiling planet.

It was born to be a shooting star but now it's laden.
So it carries a burden of fire out all across the sky.
It's a warning.

PERCY   Of war?

SAMUEL   Yes.
           I want to give you something.

           SAMUEL *passes* PERCY *something wrapped in
           a cloth.* PERCY *unwraps one corner.*

PERCY   What is it?
           What the fuck is this?
           Sam?

           SAMUEL *pushes it to* PERCY*'s chest.* PERCY
           clutches it to himself.

           The BOY *re-enters. He's leading a bent and
           cloaked* FIGURE.

BOY   My father's here to speak with you.

PERCY   Really?

BOY   This is him, Father.
           This is the one who lives on the boundary line.

PERCY   That's right.
           I want my home, sir.
           I want my name.
           I'm not anonymous, sir, I'm Percy Lamrose.
           Of Allendale.
           I live here.
           My father lived here.

BOY   He said he'd cut your fucking throat.

PERCY   No.

BOY   He's a liar, Father.
           He doesn't have a home.

PERCY   I'm Percy Lamrose, sir.
           I know it's just a map to you, sir, but it's my home.

Are you listening to me?
Sir?
I'm Percy Lamrose.

The FIGURE *staggers towards* PERCY. *It stands
in front of him. It raises its hands to lower the
hood, and whatever it is underneath lets out a
terrible scream like the lamb-beast.* SAMUEL
coughs up a gout of dark blood. PERCY *screams.*

Sudden darkness.

When the light returns the BOY *and the* FIGURE
are gone, and SAMUEL *is lying dead.* ROWAN *is
there too.* PERCY *is still clutching the unseen
object to his chest.*

The sound of distant explosions.

Fat Sam's dead.

ROWAN   Of course he is.

PERCY   I killed him.

ROWAN   I know.

PERCY   He said a war's coming.

ROWAN   He's right.

PERCY   I thought the war was over.

ROWAN   What?

PERCY   With Italy.
With Rome.
I thought it was all over.

ROWAN   What?
You thought that was the last war we'll ever have?

Like, you're the first man to be born after every
war there will ever be and it's just peace and
happiness forever and ever now?

You weren't born after the wars, you were born
between them.
You were born before them.

We are before the wars.
We're always before the wars.
The wars are always coming.
And they will take everything from you.
And from me.

The explosions sound louder now.

PERCY   Is this it for us?
         It is, isn't it?

         ROWAN *draws a knife from her belt.*

ROWAN   Yes.

         PERCY *nods.*

PERCY   Thought so.

         ROWAN *walks towards* PERCY.

         I just wanted

         I think
         I just wanted to live.

ROWAN   I know.

PERCY   But they

ROWAN   I know.

PERCY

         It's always fucking London, isn't it?

ROWAN   Yeah.
         Yeah it is.

         ROWAN *takes a step closer.*

         PERCY *holds the object he's been clutching out
         towards* ROWAN.

         It's a gun, a Mauser C96.

ROWAN *stops.*

PERCY   If you take one more step I will shoot you.

ROWAN   It starts in London.
           It starts there and it ripples.
           It ripples outwards.

           Like a stone tossed into a millpond.

           It ripples.

PERCY   I will pull this trigger and a bullet with a diameter
           of seven-point-six-three millimetres will fly
           towards your skull at a velocity of over one
           thousand feet per second / and you will die.

ROWAN   And those ripples, like broken glass, they keep
           coming.
           Again and again.
           King after king.
           And it's always us.

PERCY   You will die, say it.
           You will die.

ROWAN   It's always us.
           Always us at the edges.
           Always us, dying in the mud.
           Over and over and over again.

PERCY   He said the chain was broken.

ROWAN   It's always us.
           It's always you.
           And it's always me.

PERCY   I'll shoot you.

ROWAN   Not if I shoot you first.

           ROWAN *pulls out a modern fully automatic pistol
           and aims it at* PERCY.

           There's a bomb beneath your feet.

PERCY   Yes.

ROWAN   There are land mines all across this field.

PERCY   I know that.

          ROWAN *throws her gun away.*

ROWAN   If you take one step you die.

PERCY   I'm rigged to explode.
          I'm wearing a suicide vest.

ROWAN   My breath is contaminated with a neurotoxin.

PERCY   I carry a virus born in a laboratory and engineered
          to kill within an hour of exposure.

          ROWAN *takes out a crystal. It glows with an
          undulating white light. She holds it above her head.*

ROWAN   And if I squeeze this in my hand it will break your
          body down at a molecular level.
          Where you once were hair and bone and skin you
          will be witch hazel and the smell of burning.
          You will be the pop of Allendale air as it rushes
          into the vacuum that was once your body.
          And you will be water and you will be so much dirt
          And on the day of judgement there will be nothing
          to drag itself up and even God will not be able to
          separate you from the mud of this field.

          *The explosions are everywhere. There is a sound
          like the end of the world.*

          And then a sudden silence.

          PERCY *and* ROWAN *stare at each other, eyes
          straining. They hold for a long time. And then –*

PERCY   Is it over?

ROWAN

PERCY

          *There is a cheer in the distance. Dozens of voices
          at once.*

PERCY *and* ROWAN *freeze.*

The church bell begins to toll.

ROWAN *drops the crystal.*

Dawn begins to break.

ROWAN *and* PERCY *look out towards the sunrise.*

Would you look at that?

Pause.

The cheers are growing louder.

ROWAN   We won.

They stand in the dawn-light as the bell tolls on and on.

Blackout.

A Nick Hern Book

The Bounds first published in Great Britain in 2024 as a paperback original by Nick Hern Books Limited, The Glasshouse, 49a Goldhawk Road, London W12 8QP, in association with Live Theatre, Newcastle, and the Royal Court Theatre, London

The Bounds copyright © 2024 Stewart Pringle

Cover image by Guy J Sanders

Designed and typeset by Nick Hern Books, London
Printed in the UK by Mimeo Ltd, Huntingdon, Cambridgeshire PE29 6XX

A CIP catalogue record for this book is available from the British Library

ISBN 978 1 83904 344 4

www.nickhernbooks.co.uk/environmental-policy

www.nickhernbooks.co.uk

facebook.com/nickhernbooks

twitter.com/nickhernbooks